# Simply Ming™

# SPIRALIZER
## COOKBOOK

# Simply Ming™

# SPIRALIZER
## COOKBOOK

### SIMPLY DELICIOUS HOMEMADE RECIPES

Cover and interior design by Katie Jennings Campbell
Layout by Tara Long

Castle Point Publishing
58 Ninth Street Hoboken, NJ 07030
www.castlepointpub.com

ISBN: 978-0-9982297-2-0

Please note: Read any safety instructions that came with your spiralizer before trying any of the recipes in this book. The author, publisher, manufacturer, nor distributor can assume responsibility for the effectiveness of the recipes or text herein and shall have no liability for damages (whether direct, indirect, consequential, or otherwise) arising from the use, attempted use, misuse, or application of the described in this book.

Printed and bound in the United States of America

10 9 8 7 6 5 4 3 2 1

# CONTENTS

# WELCOME TO SPIRALIZING
## with Simply Ming

Spiralizers have gained popularity over the last few years thanks to their simple design and vast health benefits. At first glance, a spiralizer simply transforms a few basic vegetables (and fruits) into noodles. The real benefits, however, come from incorporating spiralized vegetables into your diet daily and creatively. When you let your imagination run wild with a spiralizer, you'll find yourself eating more vegetables, consuming fewer calories and even saving time in the kitchen.

## BENEFITS OF SPIRALIZING
### A SIDE-BY-SIDE ANALYSIS

Zucchini is one of the most popular vegetables to spiralize because of its strong resemblance in look and texture to traditional spaghetti when spiralized. The difference between the two nutritionally will surprise you! One medium zucchini yields roughly the same amount of "noodles" as a cup of spaghetti. The zucchini noodles (zoodles) have about 33 calories and 5 net carbs (total carbs minus fiber). A cup of spaghetti is about 220 calories and 40 net carbs. Zoodles take 3 minutes to cook while spaghetti can take around 15. See the comparison table below:

|  | 1 MEDIUM ZUCCHINI | 1 CUP SPAGHETTI |
|---|---|---|
| CALORIES | 33 | 220 |
| NET CARBS | 5 | 40 |
| COOK TIME (IN MINUTES) | 3 | 15 |

Beyond the ease and convenience of a quickly spiralized zucchini, you'd also be eating a more nutrient-dense meal. One medium zucchini has almost half of your daily vitamin C needs! It's also a good source of vitamin $B_6$.

That's just zucchini; think of all the other delicious, colorful, healthy vegetables you can incorporate into your diet with this one easy technique.

### RETAIN FLAVOR AND TEXTURE

The texture and consistency of spiralized vegetables strongly resemble those of pasta. Because flavors primarily come from the sauces and spices added to the dish, switching out an ingredient like spaghetti for zoodles is easy and very forgiving. Try the Chicken and Squash Alfredo recipe with yellow squash noodles (page 70)—you won't believe how similar it feels and tastes compared to traditional spaghetti.

### INCREASE VEGETABLE CONSUMPTION

Years of fad diets and incorrect scientific test results have come and gone. The thing that remains ingrained in our minds is "eat more vegetables," and for good reason! Vegetables are incredibly diverse and yield flavorful and nutrient-dense foods. Eating more vegetables—and taking in more vitamins, minerals and fiber—is beneficial to everyone, regardless of age, background or wellness. Eliminating processed and unnatural foods in lieu of nutrient-dense vegetables will help you feel fuller and more energized throughout your day.

### FASTER MEAL PREPARATION

Who has extra time to spare for cooking these days? Spiralizers can help reduce overall time spent in the kitchen. Spiralizing a vegetable increases the surface area by cutting it into dozens of noodles, reducing the cook time significantly. Sometimes you don't even need to cook the noodles, as many of the vegetables can be eaten raw! This means less time spent cooking and more nutrients preserved: it's a win-win.

## SPIRALIZING BASICS

### THE NOODLE SHAPES

Thanks to the unique blade system, the Simply Ming Automatic Electric Spiralizer enables you to create four different types of noodles. The blades are clearly labeled on the spiral dial.

**SETTING 1**
MAKE THICK, WIDE RIBBONS

**SETTING 2**
MAKE FETTUCCINE NOODLES
OR CURLY FRIES

**SETTING 3**
MAKE LINGUINE NOODLES

**SETTING 4**
MAKE SPAGHETTI NOODLES

## SPIRALIZER-FRIENDLY FOODS

Fruits and vegetables that are solid and relatively straight work best with your spiralizer. For example, many yellow squash can be curved at one end; try to pick one that is straight from tip to tip. The food shouldn't be hollow, as a pepper would be, but firm and whole throughout, as a zucchini, without any hard seeds or pits.

To prep your food, remove any thick peel or skin before spiralizing. For best results, food should be 1 to 3 inches in diameter and no longer than 6 inches long. Once you have your food rinsed and clean, you can trim it down (if needed) and cut it so both ends are flat.

The list below includes foods that can be spiralized and how to prepare them for spiralizing.

| ITEM | PREPARATION NEEDED FOR SPIRALIZING |
|------|-------------------------------------|
| APPLE | CORE. |
| BEET | CUT THE ENDS OFF AND PEEL. |
| BROCCOLI (STEM) | CUT THE ENDS OFF AND PEEL. |
| BUTTERNUT SQUASH | CUT OFF THE BULBOUS HALF. CUT THE END OF THE STRAIGHTER HALF OFF AND PEEL ITS HARD SKIN MULTIPLE TIMES UNTIL YOU REACH THE BRIGHT ORANGE INSIDE. |
| CABBAGE | NO PREP IS NEEDED. |
| CARROT | CUT THE ENDS OFF AND PEEL. |
| CELERIAC | CUT THE ENDS OFF AND PEEL COMPLETELY. |
| CHAYOTE | CUT THE ENDS OFF. |
| CUCUMBER | CUT THE ENDS OFF. PEELING IS OPTIONAL. |
| DAIKON RADISH | CUT THE ENDS OFF AND PEEL. |
| JICAMA | CUT THE ENDS OFF AND CAREFULLY SLICE THE WAXY SKIN OFF WITH A KNIFE. |
| PARSNIP | CUT THE ENDS OFF AND PEEL. |
| PEAR | CORE. |
| RUTABAGA | CUT THE ENDS OFF. |
| YELLOW SQUASH | CUT THE ENDS OFF. PEELING IS OPTIONAL. |
| ZUCCHINI (COURGETTE OR GREEN SQUASH) | CUT THE ENDS OFF. PEELING IS OPTIONAL. |

# ABOUT THE RECIPES
## RECIPE NOTES

We wrote the following recipe notes to clear up any confusion that may arise. Refer back to this section if needed.

**CHICKEN** In all of our recipes, we use boneless, skinless chicken breasts and boneless, skinless chicken thighs. If you have bone-in chicken thighs, be sure to debone them before preparing the recipe. If you like, you can swap out chicken breasts for chicken thighs and vice versa.

**BEEF** We prefer 85% lean ground beef. It's affordable and delicious and gives a good juiciness to the recipes. If you prefer a different percent, you can use that instead.

**SOY SAUCE** If you're gluten-free, be sure to find a gluten-free soy sauce or use tamari. Chef Ming Tsai's preferred brand is Wan Ja Shan.

**BROTH** We often use chicken broth in our recipes. Other common broths include beef, vegetable and seafood. In our recipes, we specify the broth if we think it works best with the profile of the dish. If you see just "broth" listed, feel free to use your favorite broth. Swapping vegetable broth and leaving out any meats in a soup to create a vegetarian version works just as well.

**SALT** It is important to note the difference between table salt and sea salt. Table salt is much finer while sea salt is coarse and flaky. We use sea salt in all of our recipes. If you only have table salt, you will need to reduce the amount you use in each recipe because table salt is more densely compacted in measuring spoons. Always season to taste and adjust when necessary.

**PEELING VEGETABLES** Feel free to peel any vegetables if you don't want to eat their skins. We specify which vegetables we peel (e.g., carrots and butternut squash).

## STARTER RECIPES

In a few recipes, we call for pesto or marinara sauce in the ingredients list. If you need to save time, you can always turn to prepared, store-bought options. But you might be surprised just how simple (and flavorful!) it is to make your own pesto and marinara sauce. To get you started, we've given you two recipes here.

# Classic Pesto

4 CUPS FRESH BASIL LEAVES
2 CLOVES GARLIC
1/3 CUP PINE NUTS

1/2 CUP OLIVE OIL
1/2 CUP GRATED PARMESAN CHEESE
SALT AND PEPPER

1. In a food processor or blender, combine the basil, garlic and pine nuts.
2. Add the oil, and blend until a paste forms.
3. Add the cheese and salt and pepper to taste; blend until smooth.

SIMPLE FLAVOR SWAPS

- Try some Thai basil in place of regular basil.
- Mix pine nuts with almonds.
- Replace some of the basil leaves with kale leaves.
- Toast the pine nuts.

# Fresh Marinara Sauce

2 TABLESPOONS OLIVE OIL
1/2 CUP DICED YELLOW ONION
2 CLOVES GARLIC, MINCED
1 CUP CHICKEN BROTH
1/4 CUP TOMATO PASTE
1/2 TEASPOON RED PEPPER FLAKES

1 (14.5-OUNCE) CAN SAN MARZANO
CHOPPED TOMATOES
1 TABLESPOON PARSLEY
1 TABLESPOON OREGANO
4 FRESH BASIL LEAVES, DICED
SALT AND PEPPER

1. Heat the oil in a large pan over medium heat, add the onion and cook until the onion is translucent, about 5 minutes.
2. Add the minced garlic to the pan and cook for about 1 minute longer.
3. Add 1/2 cup of the chicken broth, the tomato paste and the red pepper flakes, stirring to combine. Cook for about 3 minutes.
4. Add the tomatoes, parsley, oregano, basil and the remaining 1/2 cup chicken broth.
5. Bring to a boil. Reduce the heat and simmer uncovered for 30 minutes.
6. Add salt and pepper to taste.

SIMPLE FLAVOR SWAPS

- Swap red cooking wine in place of some of the broth.
- Try caramelizing the onions.
- Add diced carrots.

# SENSATIONAL
# SOUPS
# AND STEWS

# *Thai Basil* PARSNIP NOODLE SOUP

WAKE UP CLASSIC CHICKEN NOODLE SOUP! Thai basil, mushrooms and parsnip noodles add flavor that tastes light yet satisfies.

---

12 OUNCES BONELESS, SKINLESS CHICKEN BREASTS

2 TABLESPOONS OLIVE OIL

8 OUNCES WHITE MUSHROOMS, DICED

1 LARGE WHITE ONION, DICED

1 QUART CHICKEN BROTH

1 SPRIG THAI BASIL

SALT AND PEPPER

2 CUPS WATER

2 LARGE PARSNIPS

1. On a clean work surface, using a meat tenderizer or rolling pin, pound the chicken breasts until they are about ½ inch thick.

2. Heat 1 tablespoon of the oil in a large skillet over medium heat and sauté the breasts for 5 to 7 minutes on each side or until golden outside and the juices run clear when cut.

3. Meanwhile, heat the remaining 1 tablespoon of oil in a medium pan, add the diced mushrooms and onion and sauté over medium heat for about 5 minutes, until the onions become translucent.

4. Transfer the mushrooms and onions to a large soup pot set over medium heat.

5. Pour about ½ cup of the chicken broth into the pan you sautéed the vegetables in and use a wooden spoon to help scrape off all the caramelized bits. Pour everything from the pan into the pot as well.

6. Once the chicken breasts are fully cooked, remove them from the pan and shred them with two forks.

7. Add the chicken, Thai basil, salt and pepper to taste, water and the remaining chicken broth to the pot.

8. Trim the ends off the parsnips and peel them. With the spiralizer on setting 3, spiralize them into thick noodles. Add them to the pot.

9. Allow the soup to come to a gentle boil, reduce the heat to low and simmer for 30 to 40 minutes. Remove the Thai basil sprig and serve.

## EAT WELL *with Ming*

DID YOU KNOW JUST 1 CUP OF PARSNIPS CONTAINS ALMOST ONE-QUARTER OF YOUR DAILY FIBER NEEDS?

# Creamy Thai
# COCONUT SOUP

WITH RICH COCONUT MILK, mushrooms and zoodles, Creamy Thai Coconut Soup is a perfect meatless dinner option. You'll love the blend of sweet and spicy!

---

2 TABLESPOONS
OLIVE OIL

1-INCH CUBE GINGER,
GRATED

1 STALK LEMONGRASS

2 TABLESPOONS RED
PEPPER FLAKES

1 (15-OUNCE) CAN
COCONUT MILK

1 QUART CHICKEN OR
VEGETABLE BROTH

1 LARGE ZUCCHINI

12 OUNCES MUSHROOMS,
SLICED

1/4 CUP CHOPPED
CILANTRO

JUICE OF 1 LIME

SALT AND PEPPER

1. Heat the olive oil in a large soup pot over medium heat, add the grated ginger, lemongrass stalk and red pepper flakes and cook for 2 minutes, until fragrant.

2. Shake the can of coconut milk well. Add the coconut milk and broth to the pot.

3. Let the soup come to a boil and then lower the heat to a simmer.

4. Trim the ends off the zucchini. With the spiralizer on setting 3, spiralize it into thick noodles.

5. Add the sliced mushrooms and zoodles and cook for about 10 minutes.

6. Add the chopped cilantro and lime juice, season with salt and pepper and serve.

## EAT WELL *with Ming*

ONE CUP OF MUSHROOMS CONTAINS LARGE AMOUNTS OF COPPER AND SELENIUM, WHICH ARE EXTREMELY IMPORTANT FOR DNA PRODUCTION.

# TOMATO CABBAGE *Soup*

JUST A FEW SIMPLE STEPS give you a meal full of nutrition. The rich flavors emerge as the soup simmers.

1 HEAD GREEN CABBAGE

2 LARGE CARROTS

2 MEDIUM YELLOW ONIONS, CHOPPED

4 ROMA TOMATOES, CHOPPED

4 CLOVES GARLIC, CHOPPED

2 GREEN BELL PEPPERS, CHOPPED

2 CUPS TOMATO JUICE

1 QUART BEEF BROTH

1 QUART WATER

SALT AND PEPPER

FRESH PARSLEY, FOR GARNISH

1. With the spiralizer on setting 1, shred the head of cabbage.

2. Trim the ends off the carrots and peel them. With the spiralizer on setting 3, spiralize the carrots into thick noodles.

3. Add all the ingredients, except the parsley, to a large pot and let the soup simmer for about 45 minutes.

4. Garnish with the fresh parsley and serve warm.

## EAT WELL *with Ming*

DID YOU KNOW CABBAGE IS A GREAT SOURCE OF VITAMIN C, AN IMPORTANT ANTIOXIDANT AND AN ESSENTIAL DIETARY VITAMIN NECESSARY FOR COLLAGEN PRODUCTION?

# EGG DROP *Soup*

ORDERING EGG DROP SOUP is almost irresistible when eating at a Chinese restaurant. Now you can make this delicious Asian classic at home with restaurant-quality taste and added vegetables.

---

| 1/2 HEAD GREEN CABBAGE | 1 QUART CHICKEN BROTH | SALT AND PEPPER |
| --- | --- | --- |
| 2 MEDIUM CARROTS | 2 SCALLIONS, THINLY SLICED | 4 LARGE EGGS |

1. With the spiralizer on setting 1, shred the cabbage.

2. Trim the ends off the carrots and peel them. With the spiralizer on setting 3, spiralize them into thick noodles.

3. Heat the chicken broth in a pot over medium-high heat. Add the shredded cabbage, carrot noodles, scallion and salt and pepper to taste and bring the soup to a boil.

4. Beat the eggs in a bowl. While stirring the soup, drop in a spoonful of the eggs at a time, stirring continuously to prevent clumping.

5. Allow the soup to cook for another 5 minutes and serve.

## EAT WELL *with Ming*

EGGS ARE A GOOD SOURCE OF CHOLINE, A NUTRIENT NECESSARY FOR METABOLISM AND IMPORTANT FOR BRAIN FUNCTION.

# SAUSAGE MINESTRONE SOUP *with Broccoli Ribbons*

THE CLASSIC MINESTRONE FLAVOR with the addition of sweet Italian sausage and spiralized broccoli makes this Sausage Minestrone Soup with Broccoli Ribbons burst with savory flavors.

---

2 TABLESPOONS OLIVE OIL

8 OUNCES SPICY SAUSAGE, CASINGS REMOVED

1 MEDIUM WHITE ONION, DICED

2 STALKS CELERY, CHOPPED

1 (14.5-OUNCE) CAN WHOLE TOMATOES, DRAINED AND CHOPPED

2 MEDIUM CARROTS

2 BROCCOLI STEMS

1 QUART CHICKEN BROTH

2 CUPS WATER

1 HEAD GREEN CABBAGE

1/4 TEASPOON RED PEPPER FLAKES

1/4 TEASPOON DRIED ROSEMARY

SALT AND PEPPER

GRATED PARMESAN, FOR GARNISH

1. Heat the olive oil in a large soup pot over medium heat, add the sausage and cook until it's browned and crumbled, which should take 5 to 8 minutes.

2. Remove the sausage from the pot and transfer to a bowl, then add the onion to the pot and cook until translucent, about 5 minutes.

3. Add the chopped celery and canned tomatoes and stir to combine.

4. Trim the ends off the carrots and broccoli stems and peel them lightly. With the spiralizer on setting 1, spiralize them both into ribbons and add to the soup pot.

5. Add the chicken broth and water, bring the soup to a boil and then lower the heat to a simmer.

6. Shred the green cabbage using setting 1 on the spiralizer and add it to the simmering soup pot.

7. Add the sausage back to the pot.

8. Season the soup with the red pepper flakes, rosemary and salt and pepper to taste. Stir everything well to combine and let the soup simmer for about 20 minutes.

9. Garnish each portion with freshly grated Parmesan cheese and serve.

# *Chorizo* BUTTERNUT NOODLE SOUP

CHORIZO AND BUTTERNUT SQUASH bring a sweet symphony of flavor to your soup bowl. You can add more or less chicken broth to make the soup your preferred thickness.

4 TABLESPOONS
OLIVE OIL

2 YELLOW ONIONS,
DICED

8 CLOVES GARLIC,
MINCED

1 QUART CHICKEN BROTH

1 QUART WATER

4 (2-OUNCE)
CHORIZO LINKS

2 LARGE
BUTTERNUT SQUASH

1/2 TEASPOON
GROUND TURMERIC

1 TEASPOON PAPRIKA

1 TEASPOON GARLIC
POWDER

2 TEASPOONS
DRIED OREGANO

SALT AND PEPPER

1. Heat 2 tablespoons of the olive oil in a large soup pot over medium heat. Add the onions and garlic to the pot and cook until translucent, about 5 minutes.

2. Add the chicken broth and water, bring the soup to a boil and then lower the heat to a simmer.

3. Add the remaining 2 tablespoons olive oil to a medium pan over medium heat and sauté the chorizo links on each side for 2 minutes, until they are browned all around.

4. Remove the chorizo from the pan and slice them into ¾-inch slices. Add the chorizo slices back to the pan and cook for another 3 minutes, until they're almost fully cooked and then add them to the simmering soup pot.

5. Cut off the bulbous half from the butternut squash. Cut off the end of the straighter half and peel its hard skin multiple times until you reach the bright orange inside. With the spiralizer on setting 3, spiralize the butternut squash into thick noodles and add them to the soup.

6. Add the turmeric, paprika, garlic powder, oregano and salt and pepper to taste and continue to simmer for 30 minutes.

**EAT WELL** *with Ming*

BUTTERNUT SQUASH IS VERY HIGH IN VITAMIN A, A FAT-SOLUBLE VITAMIN IMPORTANT FOR IMMUNE FUNCTION AND VISION.

# Lemony Parsnip
# AND SALMON SOUP

THIS SOUP IS BURSTING WITH CITRUSY LEMON and zesty pepper—a great pairing with salmon. Parsnip noodles add the finishing touch.

---

1 POUND FRESH
SALMON FILLET

SALT AND CRACKED
BLACK PEPPER

3 TABLESPOONS
OLIVE OIL

1 WHITE ONION,
DICED

4 CLOVES GARLIC,
GRATED

4 MEDIUM PARSNIPS

2 CUPS VEGETABLE
BROTH

2 CUPS WATER

JUICE OF 2 LEMONS

1 TABLESPOON MISO

1 TEASPOON
GRATED GINGER

1 TEASPOON DRIED BASIL

1/2 TEASPOON RED PEPPER
FLAKES (OPTIONAL)

1. Season the salmon fillet with salt and pepper.

2. Heat 1 tablespoon of the olive oil in a large skillet over medium heat, add the salmon and fry for 5 to 7 minutes on each side or until it's pale and flakes easily with a fork.

3. Meanwhile, heat the remaining 2 tablespoons of olive oil in a soup pot over medium heat, add the onion and garlic and sauté until the onion is translucent, about 5 minutes.

4. Trim the ends off the parsnips and peel them. With the spiralizer on setting 3, spiralize them into thick noodles and add them to the soup pot. Toss the noodles to coat them in the olive oil and cook for about 2 minutes.

5. Add the vegetable broth, water, lemon juice, miso, salt to taste, 1 teaspoon pepper, ginger, basil and red pepper flakes. Stir to combine and bring the soup to a boil, then reduce the heat and let it simmer for 10 minutes.

6. Shred the cooked salmon with a fork and add it to the simmering pot. Cook for an additional 5 minutes to blend the flavors and serve.

# Simple CHICKEN PHO

NO NEED TO GRAB A RESTAURANT MENU! You can make this classic Vietnamese soup right in your own kitchen. To speed the process, look for pho soup broth at your local store.

BROTH

1 TABLESPOON SESAME OIL

1 WHITE ONION, DICED

2 CLOVES GARLIC, MINCED

1-INCH CUBE GINGER, MINCED

1 QUART CHICKEN BROTH

1/4 CUP FISH SAUCE

HOT SAUCE (OPTIONAL, SRIRACHA WORKS BEST)

1 TABLESPOON SEA SALT

1 TABLESPOON GARLIC POWDER

1/2 TABLESPOON BLACK PEPPER

1 TEASPOON GROUND CINNAMON

1 TEASPOON GROUND CORIANDER

1 TEASPOON GROUND STAR ANISE

VEGETABLES, CHICKEN AND HERBS

1 LARGE DAIKON RADISH

JUICE OF 1 LIME

12 OUNCES BONELESS, SKINLESS CHICKEN THIGHS

1 TABLESPOON OLIVE OIL

1 FRESH JALAPEÑO, SLICED (OPTIONAL)

2 SCALLIONS, CHOPPED

1 BUNCH FRESH MINT LEAVES, CHOPPED

1 BUNCH FRESH PARSLEY LEAVES, CHOPPED

BEAN SPROUTS, FOR SERVING

1.  To make the broth, heat the sesame oil in a soup pot over medium heat, add the onion and cook until it's translucent, about 5 minutes.

2.  Add the garlic and ginger and cook until they're fragrant, about 3 minutes.

3.  Add the chicken broth, fish sauce and hot sauce to taste and stir to combine.

4.  Add the salt, garlic powder, pepper, cinnamon, coriander and star anise, stir well and try a taste. Adjust the seasonings as desired and bring to a gentle boil.

5.  To make the vegetables, chicken and herbs, trim the head and end off the daikon radish and peel the outer layer. With the spiralizer on setting 4, spiralize it into thin noodles and drop

the noodles into the boiling soup. Add the lime juice and let everything cook for about 15 minutes.

6.  Meanwhile, place the chicken thighs on a clean work surface and pound them with a meat tenderizer or rolling pin until they are about ½ inch thick.

7.  Heat the olive oil in a skillet over medium-high heat, add the chicken thighs and fry for 5 to 7 minutes on each side or until golden on the outside and firm to the touch.

8.  Remove the chicken thighs from the pan and shred them with two forks.

9.  Add the shredded chicken to the broth and allow it to heat up for about 10 minutes to absorb some of the broth flavors.

10.  To serve, divide the broth among 4 bowls and garnish with the jalapeño, scallion, fresh mint, parsley and bean sprouts.

**EAT WELL** *with Ming*

DAIKON IS LOW IN CALORIES AND CARBS AND HIGH IN VITAMIN C, WHICH IS IMPORTANT FOR IMMUNE FUNCTION.

# PORK AND GREENS *Stew*

HEARTY PORK, GREENS AND VEGETABLES create a savory stew for the coldest winter nights. Warm up with a bowl!

---

2 TABLESPOONS
OLIVE OIL

1 WHITE ONION, CHOPPED

2 LARGE CARROTS,
SLICED

3 STALKS CELERY,
CHOPPED

20 OUNCES PORK
SHOULDER, CUBED

1 QUART CHICKEN
BROTH

1 QUART WATER

2 TEASPOONS SALT

2 TEASPOONS WHOLE
PEPPERCORNS

1 TEASPOON
DRIED OREGANO

1 TABLESPOON
FRESH THAI BASIL

5 BAY LEAVES

1 POUND FRESH SPINACH,
STEMMED, LEAVES
CHOPPED

1 BUTTERNUT SQUASH

1. Heat the olive oil in a large soup pot over medium heat, add the onion and cook until translucent, about 5 minutes.

2. Add the carrots and celery and let them cook for about 10 minutes, until they are a bit softened.

3. Transfer the veggies to a bowl, add the pork to the pot and sear the cubes for about a minute on all sides. This may take 2 or 3 batches, depending on the size of your soup pot.

4. Once the pork is seared, deglaze the pan by adding a bit of chicken broth and scraping some of the pieces left behind with a wooden spoon until the bottom of the soup pot is relatively clean. Add all the vegetables back in as well as the rest of the chicken broth and water.

5. Season the stew with the salt, peppercorns, oregano, basil and bay leaves and bring it to a boil.

6. Lower the heat to a simmer and add the spinach, ripping the leaves into bite-size pieces as you add them.

7. Let the soup simmer for about 3 hours, adding more water occasionally if necessary.

8. In the last 30 minutes of cooking, cut off the bulbous half of the butternut squash. Cut the end of the straighter half off and peel its hard skin multiple times until you reach the bright orange inside. With the spiralizer on setting 3, spiralize the squash into thick noodles and add them to the stew.

9. Remove the bay leaves before serving.

EAT WELL *with Ming* ─────────────────

PORK IS AN EXCELLENT SOURCE OF PROTEIN AND IS HIGH IN ZINC, AN ESSENTIAL MINERAL IMPORTANT FOR IMMUNE FUNCTION.

# FLAVORFUL
# SALADS

# *Balsamic-Marinated*
# SKIRT STEAK SALAD

GET OUT OF YOUR SOY SAUCE MARINADE RUT! Balsamic vinegar with a touch of honey makes a heavenly marinade for steak. Spiralized pears and crumbled blue cheese are the perfect flavor accents.

MARINADE AND STEAK
1/4 CUP OLIVE OIL

2 TABLESPOONS
BALSAMIC VINEGAR

2 TABLESPOONS
HONEY

1 TEASPOON SEA SALT

1/2 TEASPOON

BLACK PEPPER

24 OUNCES SKIRT STEAK

SALAD
2 PEARS

1 TEASPOON
LEMON JUICE

3 CUPS FRESH
ARUGULA

2 OUNCES ROASTED
CASHEWS (WHOLE
OR CHOPPED)

2 TABLESPOONS
OLIVE OIL

SALT

2 OUNCES BLUE CHEESE,
CRUMBLED

1. To make the marinade and steak, whisk together the oil, vinegar, honey, salt and pepper in a wide, shallow dish. Add the steak, turn to coat it with the marinade and let marinate in the refrigerator for at least 2 hours or preferably overnight.

2. Heat a skillet over medium-high heat and sear the steak for about 7 minutes on each side or until slightly pink when sliced with a knife. Transfer to a plate, cover with foil and let rest for about 5 minutes to reabsorb all its juices.

3. To make the salad, remove the stems from the pears. With the spiralizer on setting 4, spiralize them into thin noodles. Transfer the noodles to a serving bowl. Add the lemon juice to the bowl to prevent browning and toss the noodles to coat them.

4. Add the arugula and roasted cashews.

5. Dress the salad with the olive oil and salt and toss to combine.

6. Slice the skirt steak into thin strips.

7. Divide the salad among 4 plates and add the skirt steak strips equally to each.

8. Add the crumbled blue cheese on top and serve.

**EAT WELL** *with Ming*

ARUGULA IS A GREAT SOURCE OF VITAMIN K, WHICH IS IMPORTANT FOR BLOOD CLOTTING.

# *Mediterranean* CHICKEN AND BEET SALAD

LEMON, FETA, CAPERS AND CHICKEN are the greats of Greek flavor. Beets and cucumbers add fresh, crisp texture.

12 OUNCES BONELESS, SKINLESS CHICKEN BREASTS

3 TABLESPOONS OLIVE OIL

SALT AND PEPPER

2 MEDIUM BEETS

2 LARGE CUCUMBERS

JUICE OF 1 LEMON

4 OUNCES FETA CHEESE

1 TABLESPOON CAPERS, FOR GARNISH

1. Place the chicken breasts on a clean work surface and pound them with a meat tenderizer or rolling pin until they're about ½ inch thick.

2. Heat 1 tablespoon of the olive oil in a large pan over medium-high heat and sauté the chicken breasts for 5 to 7 minutes on each side or until golden on the outside and the juices run clear when cut.

3. Season with salt and pepper to taste on each side.

4. Trim any leaves and stems off the beets and peel them. Use gloves to prevent your fingers from staining. With the spiralizer on setting 4, spiralize the beets into thin noodles.

5. Cut the ends off the cucumbers. With the spiralizer on setting 2, spiralize them into thick noodles.

6. Add all the noodles to a mixing bowl and toss with the remaining 2 tablespoons of olive oil.

7. Add the freshly squeezed lemon juice and feta cheese to the mixing bowl.

8. Once the chicken breasts are ready, remove them from the pan, shred them with two forks and add them to the mix.

9. Toss the salad and divide it among 4 plates. Garnish with the capers and serve.

## EAT WELL *with Ming*

BEETS ARE LOADED WITH FOLATE, A WATER-SOLUBLE VITAMIN NECESSARY FOR PROPER DNA PRODUCTION.

# SPINACH, PEAR AND CHICKEN *Salad*

YOU'LL TASTE NOTES OF TANGY, sour and sweet in this salad. Shredding the chicken makes it easy to serve and enjoy at social gatherings.

12 OUNCES BONELESS, SKINLESS CHICKEN BREASTS

1/4 CUP OLIVE OIL

2 PEARS

2 TABLESPOONS FRESH LEMON JUICE

4 OUNCES SPINACH

1/3 CUP DRIED CRANBERRIES

SALT AND PEPPER

4 OUNCES GOAT CHEESE

1. Place the chicken breasts on a clean work surface and pound them with a meat tenderizer or rolling pin until they're about ½ inch thick.

2. Heat 1 tablespoon of the olive oil in a large pan over medium-high heat and sauté the chicken breasts for 5 to 7 minutes on each side or until golden on the outside and the juices run clear when cut.

3. Remove the chicken from the pan and shred the meat with two forks. Add the shredded chicken to a large mixing bowl.

4. Remove the stems from the pears. With the spiralizer on setting 4, spiralize them into thin noodles. Add the pear noodles to the mixing bowl.

5. Add the lemon juice, spinach, dried cranberries, salt and pepper to taste, 2 ounces of the goat cheese, crumbled, and the remaining 3 tablespoons of olive oil to the mixing bowl and toss well.

6. Divide the salad among 4 plates, crumble the remaining 2 ounces of goat cheese on top and serve.

**EAT WELL** *with Ming*

JUST 1 OUNCE OF SPINACH PROVIDES MORE THAN 100% OF YOUR DAILY TARGET FOR VITAMIN K! TALK ABOUT A SUPERFOOD!

# WALDORF SALAD

TO TAKE A TRADITIONAL CHICKEN SALAD TO THE NEXT LEVEL, try this Waldorf Salad with crisp, juicy apple noodles. It's a great take-along lunch for work or school!

1 HEART OF ROMAINE LETTUCE

1 APPLE

JUICE OF 1 LEMON

1 CUP RED GRAPES, SLICED IN HALF

½ CUP WHOLE WALNUTS

2 STALKS CELERY

12 OUNCES COOKED BONELESS, SKINLESS CHICKEN BREASTS, SHREDDED

½ CUP MAYONNAISE

SALT AND PEPPER

1. Rinse the romaine lettuce heart and slice widthwise into 1-inch strips.

2. Remove the stem from the apple. With the spiralizer on setting 4, spiralize it into thin noodles. Place the apple noodles in a bowl and squeeze a bit of lemon juice over them to prevent browning.

3. Combine the lettuce and apple noodles in a large bowl and add the grapes and walnuts.

4. Chop the celery and add it to the bowl along with the shredded chicken breast.

5. Dress the salad with the remaining lemon juice and the mayonnaise.

6. Season with salt and pepper to taste and toss very well to combine.

## EAT WELL *with Ming*

WHILE WALNUTS MAY BE HIGH IN FAT, THEY CONTAIN HIGH AMOUNTS OF ALPHA-LINOLENIC ACID, AN ESSENTIAL FATTY ACID THAT HELPS DECREASE INFLAMMATION AND MAY AID IN THE PREVENTION OF CHRONIC DISEASES.

# ASIAN TUNA SALAD
## with Avocado

LIKE A FINE STEAK, tuna is meant to be served rare. Even if you aren't the biggest fan of fish, the Asian-inspired flavors in the dish will win you over.

4 (6-OUNCE) AHI TUNA STEAKS

SALT AND PEPPER

1 TABLESPOON TOASTED SESAME OIL OR OLIVE OIL

2 MEDIUM CARROTS

2 MEDIUM CUCUMBERS

½ CUP SHELLED EDAMAME

2 AVOCADOS, PEELED, PITTED AND THINLY SLICED

¼ CUP SOY SAUCE

3 TABLESPOONS LIME JUICE

ROASTED SEAWEED, RIPPED

BLACK AND WHITE SESAME SEEDS

1. Dry the ahi tuna steaks with a paper towel and season them with salt and pepper.

2. Place a large cast-iron skillet or large deep pan over high heat. Once it's almost smoking, add the toasted sesame oil and the tuna steaks. Let them sear for about a minute or two on each side. Remove the tuna from the pan and let them rest on a plate while you prepare the rest of the salad.

3. Trim the ends off the carrots and peel them. With the spiralizer on setting 4, spiralize them into thin noodles.

4. Trim the ends off the cucumbers. With the spiralizer on setting 4, spiralize them into thin noodles.

5. Divide the noodles among 4 plates and top with an even amount of shelled edamame and ½ of an avocado.

6. Cut the tuna steaks into thin slices and place them on top of each salad.

7. Drizzle each salad with equal amounts of the soy sauce and lime juice.

8. Add the roasted seaweed shreds and season with salt and pepper to taste.

9. Garnish with the black and white sesame seeds and serve.

**EAT WELL** *with Ming*

DID YOU KNOW TUNA IS LOADED WITH BRAIN-BOOSTING VITAMINS SUCH AS NIACIN AND CHOLINE?

# *Citrus* BEET SALAD

EARTHY AND SWEET COME TOGETHER on your plate with this quick and simple salad. It'll brighten up any meal!

---

SALAD

3 BEETS

2 NAVEL ORANGES

1/2 CUP SLIVERED ALMONDS

SALT

HONEY MUSTARD VINAIGRETTE

1/4 CUP MUSTARD

1/4 CUP HONEY

1/2 CUP OLIVE OIL

2 TABLESPOONS WHITE VINEGAR

SALT AND PEPPER

1. Trim any leaves and stems off the beets and peel them. Use gloves to prevent your fingers from staining. With the spiralizer on setting 4, spiralize the beets into thin noodles and place them in a deep mixing bowl.

2. Peel the navel oranges and add the slices to the mixing bowl along with the slivered almonds. Season with salt to taste and stir to combine. Divide the salad among 4 plates.

3. To make the vinaigrette, whisk together the vinaigrette ingredients in a small bowl and drizzle it over each portion of salad. Serve immediately.

## EAT WELL *with Ming*

JUST 1/2 CUP OF SLIVERED ALMONDS CONTAINS MORE THAN HALF YOUR DAILY TARGET FOR LINOLEIC ACID, A POLYUNSATURATED ESSENTIAL FATTY ACID, IMPORTANT FOR CELL MEMBRANE STRUCTURE.

# BUFFALO CHICKEN *Slaw*

ONE NUTRITIOUS BOWL of protein and vegetables with very little prep, Buffalo Chicken Slaw could be the perfect lunch!

---

2 BONELESS, SKINLESS CHICKEN THIGHS

1 TABLESPOON OLIVE OIL

1 HEAD WHITE CABBAGE

1 LARGE CARROT

2 STALKS CELERY, CHOPPED

1/2 CUP MAYONNAISE

SALT AND PEPPER

1/4 CUP BUFFALO SAUCE

1/4 CUP BLUE CHEESE DRESSING

1. Place the chicken thighs on a clean work surface and pound them with a meat tenderizer or rolling pin until they're about 1/2 inch thick.

2. Heat the olive oil in a large pan over medium-high heat and sauté the chicken thighs for 5 to 7 minutes on each side, or until golden and firm to the touch.

3. In the meantime, with the spiralizer on setting 1, shred the cabbage. Place the cabbage in a deep mixing bowl.

4. Trim the ends off the carrot and peel it. With the spiralizer on setting 3, spiralize it into thick noodles. Cut the noodles with kitchen shears to make short segments. Add them to the shredded cabbage.

5. Add the chopped celery and mayonnaise to the cabbage. Season with salt and pepper to taste.

6. Remove the chicken thighs from the pan and shred them with two forks. Add them to the slaw.

7. Pour in the Buffalo sauce and blue cheese dressing. Toss until everything is well combined.

8. Serve the Buffalo Chicken Slaw chilled for best flavor.

## EAT WELL *With Ming*

USING CHICKEN THIGHS INSTEAD OF CHICKEN BREASTS PROVIDES A LITTLE MORE FAT TO HELP KEEP YOU FULL LONGER. IT ALSO HELPS ADD MORE FLAVOR!

# *Avocado* CHICKEN SALAD

THIS SALAD HAS IT ALL: creamy avocado, protein-packed chicken, crispy romaine and bacon, broccoli ribbons, juicy tomato and a nutty crunch.

10 OUNCES BONELESS, SKINLESS CHICKEN BREASTS

3 TABLESPOONS OLIVE OIL

1 HEART ROMAINE LETTUCE

2 BROCCOLI STEMS

1 CUP CHERRY TOMATOES

8 SLICES BACON, COOKED AND CRUMBLED

1 AVOCADO, PEELED, PITTED AND CUBED

1/2 CUP CHOPPED WALNUTS

2 TABLESPOONS WHITE VINEGAR

JUICE OF 1 LEMON

1. Place the chicken breasts on a clean work surface and pound them with a meat tenderizer or rolling pin until they're about ½ inch thick.

2. Heat 1 tablespoon of the olive oil in a large pan over medium-high heat and sauté the chicken breasts for 5 to 7 minutes on each side, or until golden on the outside and the juices run clear when cut.

3. Meanwhile, rinse the romaine and slice widthwise into 1-inch-thick slices. Add them to a mixing bowl.

4. Trim off any dry ends of the broccoli stems and peel them lightly.

With the spiralizer on setting 1, spiralize them into ribbons and add them to the mixing bowl.

5. Remove the chicken breasts from the pan and shred them with two forks.

6. Add the cherry tomatoes, shredded chicken breasts and crumbled bacon to the mixing bowl.

7. Add the avocado chunks to the mixing bowl along with the walnuts.

8. Dress the salad with the remaining 2 tablespoons olive oil, vinegar and lemon juice. Toss the ingredients gently to coat and serve.

## EAT WELL *with Ming*

AVOCADOS ARE A GOOD SOURCE OF FAT AND A GREAT SOURCE OF FIBER.

# CARROT AND DAIKON NOODLE SALAD *with Tilapia*

DAIKON AND CARROT NOODLES create a slaw texture and taste that balances the seasoned tilapia in this salad. It's a delicate dish yet filling enough to enjoy as a dinner!

1 DAIKON RADISH

1 LARGE CARROT

1 TABLESPOON PEANUT OIL

1 TEASPOON SESAME OIL

1 POUND FRESH TILAPIA

2 CAMPARI TOMATOES, DICED

JUICE OF 1 LEMON

1 TABLESPOON SOY SAUCE

SALT AND PEPPER

CHOPPED FRESH CILANTRO, FOR GARNISH

1. Trim the ends off the daikon radish and carrot and peel their top layers. With the spiralizer on setting 2 or 3, spiralize them both into thick noodles.

2. Heat the oils in a large skillet over medium heat, add the tilapia and fry on each side for 5 to 7 minutes or until it can be easily flaked with a fork and is opaque throughout.

3. During the last 5 minutes, add the daikon and carrot noodles to the pan.

4. Toss everything gently and you should see the tilapia breaking down into bite-size pieces.

5. Add the diced tomatoes to a large mixing bowl along with the lemon juice and soy sauce.

6. Add the tilapia, daikon and carrots to the mixing bowl and season everything with salt and pepper.

7. Mix everything together well, garnish the salad with the chopped fresh cilantro and serve.

## EAT WELL *with Ming*

TILAPIA IS A GREAT FISH TO COMPLEMENT THIS SALAD BECAUSE IT'S HIGH IN PROTEIN AND LOW IN FAT. IT'S SURE TO KEEP YOU FULL FOR HOURS.

# FLANK STEAK
## with Pesto Zoodles

THE PESTO IN THIS DISH uses almonds instead of pine nuts for a thicker texture and slightly different flavor. Almonds also provide more protein with less fat and fewer calories, if you're watching intake.

**STEAK AND ZOODLES**
SALT AND PEPPER

1 POUND FLANK STEAK

2 LARGE ZUCCHINI

1 TABLESPOON
OLIVE OIL

**PESTO**
1 CUP FRESH THAI BASIL,
PLUS MORE FOR GARNISH

¼ CUP SLICED ALMONDS,
PLUS MORE FOR GARNISH

1 CLOVE GARLIC

¼ CUP OLIVE OIL

1. To make the steak and zoodles, liberally season the flank steak with salt and let it sit for at least an hour. This will help tenderize the meat for a softer result.

2. Preheat the broiler and place the steak on a baking sheet about 6 inches from the heat. Depending on the thickness of the steak, it should take about 5 minutes on each side. Check the internal temperature of the steak with an instant-read thermometer; for medium-rare, the temperature should be 125°F. Remove the steak from the oven and allow it to rest on a plate at room temperature for about 5 minutes.

3. Trim the ends off the zucchini. With the spiralizer on setting 2, spiralize them into thick noodles. Heat the olive oil in a skillet over medium-low heat, add the zoodles and cook them for about 2 minutes, tossing continuously. Season the zoodles with salt and pepper to taste. Transfer the zoodles to a large bowl.

4. To make the pesto, combine the Thai basil, almonds and garlic in a food processor and blend until they are smooth.

5. While blending, slowly pour in the olive oil to create an emulsion. If you can't pour while blending, just pour in about 1 tablespoon of oil at a time and blend after each addition. Add about 2 tablespoons of the pesto to the zucchini noodles and toss to mix them together.

6. After the steak has had a chance to rest, slice it into thin strips and serve it alongside the pesto zoodles. Garnish the Steak and Almond Pesto Zoodles with the rest of the pesto, almonds and fresh basil.

**EAT WELL** *with Ming* ─────────────

USING A LEAN CUT OF STEAK SUCH AS FLANK HELPS KEEP THE PROTEIN CONTENT OF THE DISH HIGH WHILE BEING MINDFUL OF FAT CONTENT.

# WARM SQUASH, PEAR *and Greens*

SAVOR SQUASH IN ANY SEASON! Try this salad that's a firework of fresh color and flavor. To simplify prep, make the squash up to two hours ahead.

---

1 BUTTERNUT SQUASH

2 PEARS

5 TABLESPOONS OLIVE OIL

2 CUPS FRESH ARUGULA

1/2 CUP POMEGRANATE SEEDS

1/3 CUP SHELLED PUMPKIN SEEDS

1 TABLESPOON BALSAMIC VINEGAR

SALT

1. Preheat the oven to 350°F. Line a 13 x 9-inch baking sheet with aluminum foil.

2. Cut the bulbous end off of the butternut squash and then peel the outer hard skin multiple times until you get to the bright orange inside. With the spiralizer on setting 4, spiralize the squash into thin noodles.

3. Remove the stems from the pears. With the spiralizer on setting 4, spiralize them into thin noodles.

4. Combine the butternut squash noodles and pear noodles in a bowl, drizzle with 1 tablespoon of the olive oil and toss to coat.

5. Spread the noodles in an even layer on the prepared baking sheet and bake for 10 minutes. The outer edges of the noodles should be slightly browned.

6. Transfer the noodles to a mixing bowl along with the arugula, pomegranate seeds and pumpkin seeds. Toss everything to combine well.

7. Dress the salad with the remaining 4 tablespoons of olive oil, balsamic vinegar and salt to taste.

**EAT WELL** *with Ming* ────

DID YOU KNOW PUMPKIN SEEDS ARE HIGH IN MAGNESIUM AND PHOSPHOROUS?

# PORK BBQ *Salad*

PORK BARBECUE AND SPINACH-APPLE SALADS are two popular dishes to bring to picnics and potlucks. Bringing the best of their flavors together, we created a new dish. Savory pork, red onion and barbecue sauce meet fresh spinach, sweet apples and tart cranberries.

**4 CUPS SPINACH**

**1 APPLE**

**1/2 RED ONION**

**1 POUND COOKED PORK LOIN**

**2/3 CUP BARBECUE SAUCE**

**SALT AND PEPPER**

**1/2 CUP DRIED CRANBERRIES**

1. Make a bed of spinach on each of 4 plates.

2. With the spiralizer on setting 1, spiralize the apple into ribbons and arrange the ribbons nicely on the beds of spinach.

3. With the spiralizer on setting 1, spiralize the red onion half into ribbons and add the ribbons to the salad.

4. Shred the pork loin using two forks, add it to a bowl, pour in the barbecue sauce and toss to combine. Let the pork rest for a few minutes to soak up the flavors.

5. Top the salads with the pork, season with salt and pepper to taste and toss everything to combine.

6. Sprinkle the salads with the dried cranberries and serve.

**EAT WELL** *with Ming*

DID YOU KNOW JUST 1 CUP OF SPINACH HAS MORE IRON, CALCIUM, FOLATE AND VITAMINS A, C AND K THAN A SKINLESS CHICKEN BREAST?

# HERBED SALMON
## with Cucumber Ribbons

FRESH THYME BALANCES THE ACIDITY of the lemon juice in the salmon seasoning. Creamy dill dressing over cucumber salad completes the dish.

---

1 TABLESPOON OLIVE OIL

4 (8-OUNCE) SALMON FILLETS

SALT AND PEPPER

4 SPRIGS FRESH THYME

JUICE OF 1 LEMON

2 LARGE CUCUMBERS

1/4 CUP FULL-FAT GREEK YOGURT

1 TEASPOON DRIED DILL

2 TABLESPOONS CAPERS, FOR GARNISH

4 LEMON SLICES, FOR GARNISH

1. Heat the oil in a large skillet on high heat until it gets very hot.

2. Pat the salmon fillets dry and season them with salt and pepper.

3. Place the fillets skin side down in the skillet and cook them for about 5 minutes.

4. Flip each fillet and add the fresh thyme sprigs and lemon juice. Cook them for 5 more minutes or until they can be flaked easily with a fork.

5. Meanwhile, trim the ends off the cucumbers and peel them.

6. With the spiralizer on setting 1, spiralize the cucumbers into ribbons and combine them in a bowl with the yogurt, dill and salt and pepper to taste. Toss the ribbons to coat them with the dressing and divide them among 4 plates.

7. Place a fillet atop each plate of salad and garnish with the capers and lemon slices.

### EAT WELL *with Ming*

ADDING HERBS IS A FANTASTIC WAY TO PACK A LOT OF FLAVOR WITHOUT EXTRA CALORIES.

# KALE-APPLE PESTO *Salad*

KALE IS A WONDER GREEN PACKED WITH VITAMINS. You'll love it paired with crisp apple and toasted walnuts in this Kale-Apple Pesto Salad. It's a simple way to bring together amazing nutrition and taste!

---

**4 CUPS CHOPPED FRESH KALE, STEMMED**

**1/4 CUP OLIVE OIL**

**SALT AND PEPPER**

**2 GRANNY SMITH APPLES**

**1 TABLESPOON LEMON JUICE**

**2 TABLESPOONS PESTO (STORE-BOUGHT OR SEE RECIPE ON PAGE 11)**

**1/2 CUP TOASTED WALNUTS**

1. Toss the kale in a deep mixing bowl with the olive oil and a big pinch of salt. Massage the leaves with your hands for about 3 minutes to soften the kale and reduce the bitterness.

2. Remove the stem from the apples. With the spiralizer on setting 1, spiralize them into ribbons. In a small bowl, combine the apple ribbons with the lemon juice to prevent browning.

3. Add the apple ribbons, pesto, walnuts and salt and pepper to taste to the softened kale and toss to combine. Serve immediately.

## EAT WELL *with Ming* ─────────────

AN EXCELLENT SOURCE OF VITAMIN K, JUST 1 CUP OF KALE PROVIDES OVER 500% OF YOUR DAILY TARGET! MASSAGING THE KALE HELPS SOFTEN IT AND REMOVE SOME OF ITS BITTERNESS.

# FRUIT AND ARUGULA SALAD *with Lemon Vinaigrette*

THE TANGY LEMON VINAIGRETTE really makes the flavors of the berries and apple shine. You can enjoy this salad year-round, but the flavor is best when the fruit is in season.

SALAD

4 CUPS FRESH ARUGULA

2 CUPS SLICED STRAWBERRIES

1 CUP BLUEBERRIES

1 APPLE

1/2 RED ONION

LEMON VINAIGRETTE

JUICE OF 1/2 LEMON

2 TABLESPOONS BALSAMIC VINEGAR

1 TEASPOON SEA SALT

1/2 TEASPOON PEPPER

1/4 CUP OLIVE OIL

1. Add the arugula, sliced strawberries and blueberries to a deep mixing bowl.

2. Remove the stem from the apple. With the spiralizer on setting 1, spiralize it into ribbons. Add it to the bowl.

3. With the spiralizer on setting 1, spiralize the red onion into ribbons and add them to the bowl.

4. To make the lemon vinaigrette, combine the lemon juice, vinegar, salt and pepper in a small bowl and whisk it all together.

5. While whisking, drizzle in the olive oil slowly to form an emulsion.

6. Drizzle the salad with the vinaigrette and serve.

EAT WELL *with Ming*

JUST 1 CUP OF STRAWBERRIES HAS MORE THAN 100% OF YOUR DAILY TARGET FOR VITAMIN C!

# LIME SHRIMP AND AVOCADO *Salad*

THIS REFRESHING SALAD is sure to become a new favorite! It's just the right combination of sweet and spicy—and comes together quickly.

SHRIMP
1 TABLESPOON OLIVE OIL

12 OUNCES LARGE SHRIMP

1/2 TEASPOON PAPRIKA

PINCH OF CAYENNE (OPTIONAL)

JUICE OF 1/2 LIME

SALT AND PEPPER

SALAD
1 MEDIUM CUCUMBER

1 MEDIUM CARROT

1/4 CUP MAYONNAISE

1 TABLESPOON SOY SAUCE

2 TEASPOONS SRIRACHA (OPTIONAL)

1 AVOCADO, PEELED, PITTED AND DICED

SALT AND PEPPER

1. To make the shrimp, heat the olive oil in a large pan over high heat. Add the shrimp and cook for 3 to 4 minutes on each side, until they are completely pink and opaque.

2. Season the shrimp with the paprika, cayenne, lime juice and salt and pepper to taste. Stir to coat the shrimp fully and then remove the pan from the heat.

3. To make the salad, trim the ends off the cucumber and carrot; peel.

4. With the spiralizer on setting 4, spiralize both vegetables into thin noodles, transfer to a mixing bowl and add the mayonnaise, soy sauce, sriracha and diced avocado. Season with salt and pepper to taste and toss gently to combine.

5. Add the cooked shrimp and toss gently again.

6. Divide the salad among 4 plates and serve.

## EAT WELL *with Ming*

DID YOU KNOW SHRIMP IS LOADED WITH VITAMIN $B_{12}$ AND PHOSPHOROUS? BOTH ARE IMPORTANT NUTRIENTS THAT AID IN DNA PRODUCTION.

# PULLED PORK AND APPLE *Salad*

CREAMY, MEATY AND CRUNCHY TEXTURES come together for a satisfying salad. The lemony vinaigrette adds a little zest.

---

SALAD
4 CUPS FRESH ARUGULA

1 FUJI APPLE

2 AVOCADOS, CORED, PEELED AND SLICED

12 OUNCES COOKED PULLED PORK

2 OUNCES PECANS, CRUSHED OR WHOLE

LEMON VINAIGRETTE
JUICE OF 1/2 LEMON

2 TABLESPOONS BALSAMIC VINEGAR

1 TEASPOON SALT

1/2 TEASPOON PEPPER

1/4 CUP OLIVE OIL

1. To make the salad, arrange the arugula in a bed on each of 4 plates.

2. Remove the stem from the apple. With the spiralizer on setting 1, spiralize it into ribbons. Arrange the ribbons nicely on the beds of arugula.

3. Lay out half an avocado in slices on each plate.

4. Add the pulled pork to each serving and sprinkle the pecans on top.

5. To make the vinaigrette, combine the lemon juice, vinegar, salt and pepper in a small bowl and whisk to blend. While whisking, drizzle in the olive oil slowly to form an emulsion.

6. Drizzle the Pulled Pork and Apple Salad with the Lemon Vinaigrette and serve.

## EAT WELL *with Ming*

USING APPLES IN SALADS IS A GREAT WAY TO INCREASE FIBER AND ADD A TOUCH OF SWEETNESS BY USING NATURAL SUGARS INSTEAD OF TABLE SUGAR IN SALAD DRESSINGS.

# Sesame Ginger
# SALMON SALAD

TAKE YOUR SALAD GAME TO A NEW LEVEL with bright Asian flavors. This salmon salad features a delicious mix of creamy avocado, salty soy sauce and sweet and spicy ginger.

---

2 TABLESPOONS OLIVE OIL

12 OUNCES SALMON FILLETS

2 MEDIUM CUCUMBERS

2 MEDIUM CARROTS

1/2-INCH CUBE GINGER, GRATED

1 TABLESPOON SOY SAUCE

2 AVOCADOS, PEELED, PITTED AND SLICED

BLACK AND WHITE SESAME SEEDS, FOR GARNISH

1. Heat the olive oil in a large skillet over medium heat, add the salmon and fry for 4 to 6 minutes on each side, depending on thickness of the fillets. They should flake easily with a fork.

2. Trim the ends off the cucumbers. With the spiralizer on setting 4, spiralize them into thin noodles.

3. Trim the ends off the carrots and peel them. With the spiralizer on setting 4, spiralize them into thin noodles.

4. Add the grated ginger, carrot noodles and cucumber noodles to a mixing bowl and drizzle them with the soy sauce. Toss to coat everything evenly and divide the salad among 4 plates.

5. Shred the cooked salmon with a fork and sprinkle an equal portion onto each salad.

6. Add half a sliced avocado to each plate and garnish with the black and white sesame seeds.

## EAT WELL with Ming

DID YOU KNOW GINGER IS ONE OF CHEF TSAI'S FAVORITE AROMATICS? IN ADDITION TO ITS GREAT FLAVOR, GINGER CAN HELP REDUCE NAUSEA AND VOMITING DUE TO COMPOUNDS THAT ASSIST WITH PROCESSES IN THE GI TRACT.

# STRAWBERRY ARUGULA SALAD *with Pecans*

THERE'S A REASON STRAWBERRY-PECAN SALADS POP up on tons of restaurant menus! When sweet strawberries meet fresh greens and salty pecans, it's flavor perfection.

2 MEDIUM CUCUMBERS

2 CUPS FRESH ARUGULA

8 OUNCES STRAWBERRIES, SLICED

2 OUNCES GOAT CHEESE

2 OUNCES ROASTED AND SALTED PECANS

1 TABLESPOON CHIA SEEDS

1 TO 2 TABLESPOONS MILD-FLAVORED OIL (SUCH AS AVOCADO)

1 TO 2 TABLESPOONS BALSAMIC VINEGAR

1. Trim the ends off the cucumbers. With the spiralizer on setting 1, spiralize them into ribbons. Place the ribbons in a mixing bowl along with the arugula. You may want to cut the cucumber ribbons into smaller strips.

2. Add the sliced strawberries and crumble the goat cheese over the top.

3. Add the pecans and chia seeds, drizzle the salad with the oil and vinegar, toss the ingredients gently to combine and serve.

## EAT WELL *with Ming*

CHIA SEEDS ARE INCREDIBLY POWERFUL BURSTS OF NUTRITION! THEY ARE VERY HIGH IN ALPHA-LINOLEIC ACID, WHICH IS AN ESSENTIAL FATTY ACID HELPFUL FOR RAISING HDL CHOLESTEROL (THE GOOD KIND!).

# GINGER CARROT *Salad*

FRESH GINGER AND SESAME OIL pack a lot of flavor into this simple salad. It's crispy, colorful and bursting with Asian zest.

SALAD
2 MEDIUM CARROTS

2 MEDIUM CUCUMBERS

1 RADISH

½ CUP SHELLED EDAMAME

DRESSING
JUICE OF 1 LIME

1 TABLESPOON SESAME OIL (OR OLIVE OIL)

1 TABLESPOON SOY SAUCE

1 INCH CUBE GINGER, GRATED

SALT AND PEPPER

GARNISH
2 SHEETS ROASTED SEAWEED, CHOPPED

2 SCALLIONS, CHOPPED

1. Trim the ends off the carrots and peel them. With the spiralizer on setting 4, spiralize them into thin noodles. Add the noodles to a salad bowl.

2. Trim the ends off the cucumbers. With the spiralizer on setting 4, spiralize them into thin noodles. Add the cucumber noodles to the salad bowl.

3. Cut the radish into thin slices and add it to the salad bowl along with the shelled edamame.

4. Combine the dressing ingredients in a small mixing bowl and whisk together until combined.

5. Dress the salad and toss well to coat everything.

6. Divide the salad among 4 plates and garnish with a few pieces of roasted seaweed and a scattering of scallions.

## EAT WELL *with Ming*

EDAMAME IS WONDERFUL ADDITION TO THIS SALAD. DID YOU KNOW IT'S HIGH IN FOLATE, A VITAMIN THAT IS EXTREMELY IMPORTANT IN DNA PRODUCTION?

# FUJI APPLE, CHICKEN AND KALE *Salad*

BOLD FLAVORS AND HEARTY KALE make this salad a great choice for cooler days.

12 OUNCES BONELESS, SKINLESS CHICKEN BREASTS

2 TABLESPOONS OLIVE OIL

8 OUNCES FRESH KALE

JUICE OF 1 LEMON

PINCH OF SALT

1 FUJI APPLE

1 TABLESPOON APPLE CIDER VINEGAR

2 OUNCES FETA CHEESE

1/4 CUP PINE NUTS

1. Place the chicken breasts on a clean work surface and pound them with a meat tenderizer or rolling pin until they're about ½ inch thick.

2. Heat 1 tablespoon of the olive oil in a large pan over medium-high heat and sauté the chicken for 5 to 7 minutes on each side, or until golden outside and the juices run clear.

3. In the meantime, place the kale in a deep mixing bowl, drizzle with the lemon juice, remaining 1 tablespoon olive oil and a big pinch of salt. Massage the leaves with your hands for about 2 minutes to soften the kale and reduce the bitterness.

4. With the spiralizer on setting 1, spiralize the apple into ribbons and add a squirt of lemon juice to prevent browning.

5. Remove the chicken breasts from the pan and shred them with two forks.

6. Add the apple ribbons, shredded chicken and a pinch of salt to the kale salad. Drizzle with the apple cider vinegar and toss to combine the ingredients.

7. Crumble the feta cheese into the bowl, sprinkle on the pine nuts for extra texture and crunch and serve.

**EAT WELL** *with Ming*

WATERCRESS IS HIGH IN VITAMIN K, KEY FOR BLOOD CLOTTING AND BONE HEALTH.

# PESTO CHICKEN
## Butternut Ribbon Salad

BOLD BASIL PESTO AND TANGY MAYONNAISE come together to create a new type of sauce in this Pesto Chicken Butternut Ribbon Salad. It's a simply delicious lunch or dinner!

PESTO
1 CUP FRESH
BASIL LEAVES

2 TABLESPOONS
PINE NUTS

2 TABLESPOONS GRATED
PARMESAN CHEESE

1 CLOVE GARLIC

SALT AND PEPPER

¼ CUP OLIVE OIL

NOODLES AND CHICKEN
2 BUTTERNUT SQUASH

1 POUND BONELESS,
SKINLESS CHICKEN
THIGHS

2 TABLESPOONS
OLIVE OIL

3 LARGE ROMA
TOMATOES, DICED

¼ CUP MAYONNAISE

1 TEASPOON DRIED BASIL,
FOR GARNISH

1. Preheat the oven to 450°F. Line a 13 x 9-inch baking sheet with foil and grease the foil.

2. To make the pesto, combine the basil, pine nuts, Parmesan, garlic and salt and pepper to taste in a food processor and blend until smooth.

3. While blending, slowly pour in the olive oil to create an emulsion. If you can't pour while blending, just pour in about 1 tablespoon of olive at a time and blend after each addition.

4. To make the noodles and chicken, cut off the bulbous half of the butternut squash. Cut the end of the straighter half off and peel its hard skin multiple times until you reach the bright orange inside. With the spiralizer on setting 1, spiralize the squash into ribbons.

5. Spread the ribbons on the prepared baking sheet and bake them for 15 minutes to deepen their flavor. The outer edges of the ribbons should be slightly browned.

6. Meanwhile, place the chicken thighs on a clean work surface and pound them with a meat tenderizer or rolling pin until they're about ½ inch thick.

7. Heat the olive oil in a large pan over medium-high heat and sauté the chicken thighs for 5 to 7 minutes on each side, or until they are golden and firm to the touch.

8. Remove the chicken from the pan, shred the meat with two forks and add it to a deep mixing bowl along with the squash ribbons.

9. Add the diced tomatoes, pesto and mayonnaise to the bowl. Toss everything very well to combine.

10. Garnish with the dried basil and serve.

**EAT WELL** *with Ming*

TOMATOES ARE A GREAT SOURCE OF LYCOPENE, A PIGMENT THOUGHT TO HAVE MANY ANTIOXIDANT PROPERTIES.

# AMAZING MAINS

# Chicken and Squash ALFREDO

WANT TO SNEAK A LITTLE EASY NUTRITION into your chicken alfredo? Just swap spiralized yellow squash for those pasta noodles. You'll gain new flavor and a nutrition edge!

**CHICKEN AND NOODLES**
1 POUND BONELESS, SKINLESS CHICKEN BREASTS

1 TABLESPOON OLIVE OIL

2 LARGE YELLOW SQUASH

8 FRESH BASIL LEAVES, FOR GARNISH

**ALFREDO SAUCE**
4 TABLESPOONS UNSALTED BUTTER

4 CLOVES GARLIC, CRUSHED

1/2 CUP HEAVY CREAM

6 TABLESPOONS GRATED PARMESAN CHEESE, PLUS MORE FOR GARNISH

SALT AND PEPPER

1. To make the chicken and noodles, place the chicken breasts on a clean work surface and pound them with a meat tenderizer or rolling pin until they're about ½ inch thick.

2. Heat the olive oil in a large pan over medium heat and sauté the chicken breasts for 5 to 7 minutes on each side or until golden on the outside and the juices run clear when cut. Remove the chicken from the pan and transfer them to a plate while you prepare the sauce and noodles.

3. To make the sauce, in the same pan, melt the butter over low heat and then add the crushed garlic and heavy cream. Let this simmer for 3 minutes.

4. Add the Parmesan cheese 1 tablespoon at a time, waiting until each is incorporated, while mixing continuously. Season with salt and pepper and let the sauce simmer for an additional 5 minutes. The sauce should be pretty thick at this point.

5. Trim the ends off of the yellow squash. With the spiralizer on setting 2, spiralize them into thick noodles. Add the squash noodles to the pan and cook in the sauce for about 5 minutes.

6. Shred the chicken breast with two forks and add it to the pan. Toss everything to coat it in the sauce.

7. Garnish the Chicken Squash Alfredo with more Parmesan cheese and chopped fresh basil.

EAT WELL *with Ming*

DID YOU KNOW GARLIC HAS ANTIOXIDANT PROPERTIES THAT CAN HELP PROTECT AGAINST CERTAIN CANCERS? USE IT IN THIS `PASTA` DISH AS A DELICIOUS AROMATIC IN THE SAUCE!

# GINGER CHICKEN *Stir-Fry*

MAGIC HAPPENS when fresh vegetables hit the pan with toasted sesame oil, ginger and soy sauce. It's a quick, healthy, satisfying dinner!

1 POUND BONELESS, SKINLESS CHICKEN BREASTS

2 TABLESPOONS OLIVE OIL

1/2-INCH CUBE GINGER, GRATED

1 HEAD OF BROCCOLI WITH STEM

2 MEDIUM CARROTS

1 RED BELL PEPPER

1 YELLOW BELL PEPPER

2 TABLESPOONS TOASTED SESAME OIL

1/4 CUP SOY SAUCE

1 TABLESPOON SESAME SEEDS

1 TABLESPOON CHOPPED FRESH PARSLEY

1. Cut the chicken breasts into cubes. Place the cubes in a baking dish, add 1 tablespoon of olive oil and ginger, cover with plastic wrap, transfer to the refrigerator and let them marinate for at least 4 hours or overnight if possible.

2. Heat a skillet over medium heat and add 1 tablespoon of olive oil. Drain the marinated chicken, add it to the pan and cook for about 10 minutes, tossing the cubes to cook on all sides until they are cooked through. Remove the chicken from the pan and shred it with two forks.

3. Meanwhile, cut off the broccoli stem from the florets. Cut off any dry ends and lightly peel the stem.

4. Trim the ends off the carrots and peel them.

5. With the spiralizer on setting 4, spiralize the broccoli stem and the carrots into thin noodles.

6. Cut the remaining broccoli into small florets and chop the red and yellow bell peppers into thin strips.

7. Add the sesame oil (or more olive oil), broccoli florets, broccoli noodles, carrot noodles and peppers to the pan and cook over high heat for about 10 minutes, stirring occasionally.

8. In the last 2 minutes, add the soy sauce and the cooked, shredded chicken to the pan and stir to combine and coat all the ingredients with the sauce.

9. Garnish with the sesame seeds and fresh parsley and serve.

**EAT WELL** *with Ming*

DID YOU KNOW THAT JUST 1 CUP OF BROCCOLI FLORETS NOT ONLY PROVIDES YOU WITH A GREAT SOURCE OF FIBER BUT IS ALSO A GOOD SOURCE OF VITAMINS C AND K?

# CHICKEN NOODLE BOWL
## with Tahini Dressing

TAHINI IS SIMPLY GROUND SESAME SEEDS that resemble a nut butter. It adds a creaminess and sesame flavor that is perfect for dressings, like in this Chicken Noodle Bowl.

**CHICKEN AND NOODLES**

24 OUNCES BONELESS, SKINLESS CHICKEN BREASTS

2 TABLESPOONS OLIVE OIL

2 LARGE PARSNIPS

**TAHINI DRESSING**

¼ CUP TAHINI

2 TEASPOONS HONEY

JUICE OF ½ LIME

2 CLOVES GARLIC

1 TEASPOON GRATED GINGER

2 TABLESPOONS OLIVE OIL

2 TABLESPOONS WATER

SALT AND PEPPER

SESAME SEEDS, FOR GARNISH

1. Place the chicken breasts on a clean work surface and pound them with a meat tenderizer or rolling pin until they're about ½ inch thick.

2. Heat 1½ tablespoons of the olive oil in a large pan over medium-high heat and sauté the chicken breasts for 5 to 7 minutes on each side or until golden on the outside and the juices run clear when cut. Transfer the chicken to a bowl and shred the meat using two forks.

3. Meanwhile, trim the ends off the parsnips and peel them. With the spiralizer on setting 3, spiralize them into thick noodles.

4. Heat the remaining ½ tablespoon of oil in a skillet over medium heat, add the parsnip noodles and cook for 4 to 5 minutes, or until they are cooked to your preference.

5. To make the tahini dressing, add the tahini, honey, lime juice, garlic, ginger, oil, water and salt and pepper to taste to a food processor and blend the ingredients until you get a smooth consistency.

6. Place the shredded chicken, parsnip noodles and tahini dressing in a bowl and toss to combine.

7. Garnish with the sesame seeds and serve.

## EAT WELL *with Ming*

USING TAHINI, A SESAME SEED PASTE, IS A SIMPLE AND EASY WAY TO MAKE A NUT-FREE NOODLE BOWL. ADDITIONALLY, TAHINI IS HIGHER IN FIBER AND LOWER IN TOTAL FAT AND SUGARS IN COMPARISON TO STANDARD GROCERY STORE PEANUT BUTTER.

# *Cheesy* BROCCOLI CHICKEN BAKE

LOOKING FOR AN EASY DINNER the whole family will love? This Cheesy Broccoli Chicken Bake is super easy to make and kid-friendly.

---

3 TABLESPOONS OLIVE OIL

4 BROCCOLI STEMS

1 HEAD BROCCOLI

12 OUNCES BONELESS, SKINLESS CHICKEN BREASTS

2 TABLESPOONS UNSALTED BUTTER

1/2 MEDIUM WHITE ONION, CHOPPED

1/2 CUP HEAVY CREAM

2 TEASPOONS DIJON MUSTARD

SALT AND PEPPER

10 OUNCES SHARP WHITE CHEDDAR CHEESE, SHREDDED, DIVIDED

CHOPPED FRESH PARSLEY, FOR GARNISH

1. Preheat the oven to 350°F. Grease a 13 x 9-inch casserole dish with 1 tablespoon of the olive oil.

2. Trim the ends off the broccoli stems and peel them. With the spiralizer on setting 2 or 3, spiralize them into thick noodles.

3. Chop the head of broccoli into florets.

4. Place the chicken breasts on a clean work surface and pound them with a meat tenderizer or rolling pin until they're about 1/2 inch thick.

5. Heat the remaining 2 tablespoons olive oil in a large skillet over medium heat and sauté the chicken breasts for 5 to 7 minutes on each side, or until golden on the outside and the juices run clear when cut. Remove the breasts from the pan, shred them with two forks and set the chicken aside.

6. In the same pan, melt the butter and then add the chopped onion and broccoli florets. Sauté for 2 minutes and then add the heavy cream. Stir the cream continuously and add the Dijon mustard and salt and pepper to taste and cook the mixture until it starts to thicken.

7. Remove the sauce from the heat and stir in 8 ounces of the shredded cheddar cheese until it fully melts.

8. Add the broccoli cheese sauce, shredded chicken and broccoli noodles to the prepared casserole dish. Stir to combine all the ingredients well.

9. Cover the dish with foil and bake for 20 minutes.

10. Uncover the dish and sprinkle the remaining 2 ounces shredded cheddar cheese evenly over the top. Bake the dish for another 10 minutes, or until the cheese browns.

11. Remove the dish from the oven, garnish with the fresh parsley and serve.

**EAT WELL** *with Ming* ——————————

WHILE IT'S IMPORTANT TO TAKE SERVING SIZE INTO ACCOUNT DUE TO HIGH FAT CONTENT, CHEESE IS A GREAT SOURCE OF CALCIUM AND PHOSPHOROUS, BOTH IMPORTANT FOR BONE HEALTH.

# Chicken Parmesan ZOODLES

CHICKEN PARMESAN IS AN OLD FAVORITE, but there is so much new you can bring to the dish. Try grated Parmesan cheese as a flavorful breading for chicken, and bring new nutrition with spiralized zucchini.

1 POUND BONELESS, SKINLESS CHICKEN BREASTS

2 MEDIUM EGGS

1/2 CUP GRATED PARMESAN CHEESE

1 TEASPOON DRIED BASIL

1 TEASPOON DRIED OREGANO

1 TEASPOON GARLIC POWDER

CRUSHED RED PEPPER FLAKES (OPTIONAL)

SALT AND PEPPER

4 ZUCCHINI

1 TABLESPOON OLIVE OIL

4 CLOVES GARLIC, CHOPPED

2 CUPS MARINARA SAUCE

2 OUNCES FRESH MOZZARELLA CHEESE

FRESH BASIL, FOR GARNISH

1. Preheat the oven to 400°F. Line a 13 x 9-inch baking sheet with foil and grease the foil.

2. Place the chicken breasts on a clean work surface and pound them with a meat tenderizer or rolling pin until they're ½ to ¾ inch thick.

3. Crack the eggs into a large bowl and whisk them with a fork.

4. In a small bowl, combine the Parmesan cheese, dried basil, oregano, garlic powder, red pepper flakes, if using, and salt and pepper to taste and spread the mixture evenly on a large, shallow plate.

5. Dredge each chicken breast in the beaten eggs and then press gently into the Parmesan cheese mixture. Make sure each breast is fully coated in the "breading."

6. Place each coated breast on the prepared baking sheet and bake for 20 minutes.

7. Meanwhile, trim the ends off the zucchini. With the spiralizer on setting 1, spiralize them into thin noodles.

8. Heat the olive oil in a pan over medium heat. Add the chopped garlic and cook for 3 minutes, then add the noodles and cook them for 2 minutes, tossing continuously.

9. Add 1 cup of the marinara sauce and let it simmer for 5 minutes.

10. Slice the fresh mozzarella into as many pieces as you have chicken.

11. When the chicken has 5 minutes remaining, take the baking sheet out and add the fresh mozzarella slices to each chicken breast, and then ladle the remaining 1 cup of marinara evenly over the top of each chicken breast. Put the chicken breasts back into the oven to finish cooking.

12. Serve the chicken on top of the zoodles and garnish with the fresh basil leaves.

## EAT WELL *with Ming*

BY USING PARMESAN CHEESE AS THE BREADING IN THIS RECIPE, YOU NOT ONLY DECREASE CARBOHYDRATE INTAKE, BUT YOU ALSO GET ALL THE DELICIOUS TANGY FLAVOR OF THE CHEESE. ADD IN CRUSHED RED PEPPER FLAKES ALONG WITH ALL THE HERBS TO TAKE IT UP A NOTCH!

# *Chicken* PAD THAI

ZOODLES ADD A NEW TWIST TO AN ASIAN CLASSIC. You can also try variations on this recipe with shrimp or tofu instead of chicken.

1 TABLESPOON OLIVE OIL

1 WHITE ONION, ROUGHLY CHOPPED

2 CLOVES GARLIC, MINCED

1 POUND BONELESS, SKINLESS CHICKEN THIGHS

SALT AND PEPPER

2 ZUCCHINI

1 LARGE EGG

2 TABLESPOONS SOY SAUCE

1/2 TEASPOON RED PEPPER FLAKES (OPTIONAL)

1 OUNCE PEANUTS, CRUSHED OR WHOLE

1 LIME, CUT INTO WEDGES

1.  Heat the olive oil in a wok or large pan over medium heat, add the chopped onion and cook until it is translucent, 5 to 6 minutes. Add the garlic and cook until it is fragrant, about 3 minutes.

2.  Season the chicken thighs with salt and pepper and place them in the wok. Let them cook for 5 to 7 minutes on each side, or until fully cooked.

3.  Remove the chicken thighs from the wok and shred them using two forks.

4.  Trim the ends off the zucchini. With the spiralizer on setting 1, spiralize them into thin noodles. Set the noodles aside.

5.  Create a well in the center of the wok and crack an egg into it. Allow it to cook for a few seconds and then scramble it into large chunks.

6.  Add the zucchini noodles to the pan. Let the noodles cook for just about 2 minutes, tossing continuously.

7.  Add the shredded chicken and finish it all off with the soy sauce, lime juice and red pepper flakes, if using.

8.  Top the Chicken Pad Thai with the peanuts and serve with the lime wedges alongside the dish.

USING RED PEPPER FLAKES AND LIME JUICE HELPS ADD GREAT FLAVOR TO A DISH WITHOUT ADDING EXTRA CALORIES, FAT AND SODIUM. ALSO, USING SOY SAUCE INSTEAD OF EXTRA SALT HELPS DECREASE SODIUM.

# Greek Chicken
# ZOODLE SALAD

YOU CAN FEEL GOOD about eating this refreshing salad packed with flavorful vegetables and lean protein. Make a bigger batch to take and share at social gatherings—it's sure to disappear!

12 OUNCES BONELESS, SKINLESS CHICKEN BREASTS

4 TABLESPOONS OLIVE OIL

4 CAMPARI TOMATOES, DICED

1/2 MEDIUM WHITE ONION, DICED

JUICE OF 1 LEMON

2 OUNCES PITTED OLIVES

1 OUNCE CAPERS

2 MEDIUM CUCUMBERS

2 MEDIUM ZUCCHINI

4 OUNCES FETA CHEESE

CHOPPED FRESH PARSLEY, FOR GARNISH

1. Place the chicken breasts on a clean work surface and pound them with a meat tenderizer or rolling pin until they're about ½ inch thick.

2. Heat 2 tablespoons of the olive oil in a large pan over medium heat and sauté the chicken breasts for 5 to 7 minutes on each side or until golden on the outside and the juices run clear when cut.

3. Meanwhile, add the diced tomatoes and onion to a large mixing bowl along with the lemon juice, olives, capers and remaining 2 tablespoons of olive oil.

4. Trim the ends off the cucumbers and peel them. With the spiralizer on setting 3, spiralize them into thick noodles. Add the noodles to the mixing bowl.

5. Remove the chicken from the pan and shred it using two forks. Add the shredded chicken to the mixing bowl.

6. Trim the ends off the zucchini. With the spiralizer on setting 3, spiralize them into thick noodles.

7. Lightly cook the zoodles in the same pan for 2 minutes and then add them to the mixing bowl.

8. Crumble the feta cheese into the mixing bowl and toss well.

9. Garnish the salad with the fresh parsley and serve.

## EAT WELL *with Ming*

DID YOU KNOW CUCUMBERS ARE MOSTLY MADE UP OF WATER? USE THEM SPIRALIZED IN THIS GREEK CHICKEN ZOODLE SALAD AS A GREAT LOW-CARB ALTERNATIVE TO PASTA AND REAP THEIR HYDRATING BENEFITS!

# CREAMY TARRAGON CHICKEN *with Broccoli Ribbons*

THIS DINNER DISH uses fewer than ten ingredients but looks and tastes impressive with its slightly sweet, creamy sauce.

4 (4-OUNCE) BONELESS, SKINLESS CHICKEN THIGHS

SALT AND PEPPER

2 TABLESPOONS OLIVE OIL

4 LARGE BROCCOLI HEADS WITH STEMS

SAUCE
1 TABLESPOON OLIVE OIL

½ WHITE ONION, CHOPPED

1 CUP FULL-FAT GREEK YOGURT

1 TABLESPOON FRESH TARRAGON

SALT AND PEPPER

1. Place the chicken thighs on a clean work surface and pound them with a meat tenderizer or rolling pin until they're about ½ inch thick. Season both sides of the chicken with salt and pepper.

2. Heat 1 tablespoon of the olive oil in a large pan over medium heat and sauté the chicken thighs for about 4 minutes on each side, until almost fully cooked. Set the thighs aside on a plate to rest while you prepare the sauce.

3. To make the sauce, heat the olive oil in a skillet over medium heat, add the chopped onion and cook until it turns translucent, 5 to 6 minutes. Lower the heat and add the yogurt and tarragon. Add salt and pepper to taste. Stir to combine everything and let it simmer for about 2 minutes.

4. Add the chicken thighs to the pan with the sauce and cook for about 10 minutes. Flip the chicken thighs a few times to make sure they're well coated in the sauce.

5. Meanwhile, separate the broccoli heads from the stems. Trim off any dry ends from the stems and peel them. With the spiralizer on setting 1, spiralize the stems into thin noodles.

6. Heat the remaining 1 tablespoon olive oil in a skillet, add the noodles and about 2 cups of the broccoli florets, season with salt and pepper and cook for about 5 minutes, tossing continuously. The noodles should soften and the florets should turn a brighter green with the edges slightly brown.

7. Serve the creamy tarragon chicken thighs on top of the cooked broccoli noodles. Add a few broccoli florets to each plate as well.

EAT WELL *with Ming*

USING FULL-FAT GREEK YOGURT INSTEAD OF SOUR CREAM HELPS INCREASE THE PROTEIN CONTENT OF THE DISH. DON'T BE AFRAID OF THE FULL FAT CONTENT—IT HELPS YOU FEEL FULLER LONGER, AND A LITTLE GOES A LONG WAY!

# CHICKEN PAPRIKASH
## with Squash Noodles

THIS CREAMY DISH LOOKS BEAUTIFUL, and the recipe could easily be doubled to please a crowd. You can serve it right from the cast-iron skillet you prepare it in!

---

2 TABLESPOONS OLIVE OIL

1/2 MEDIUM WHITE ONION, DICED

4 CLOVES GARLIC, MINCED

2 TEASPOONS PAPRIKA

SALT AND PEPPER

2 ROMA TOMATOES, DICED

1 MEDIUM RED BELL PEPPER, DICED

1 CUP CHICKEN BROTH

1 POUND BONELESS, SKINLESS CHICKEN THIGHS

2 LARGE YELLOW SQUASH

1/4 CUP WHOLE MILK

1. Heat 1 tablespoon of the olive oil in a cast-iron skillet over medium heat, add the onion and cook until it is translucent, about 5 minutes. Add the garlic and cook for an additional 2 minutes, or until it is fragrant.

2. Add the paprika and season with salt and pepper. Mix everything until the onion and garlic are fully coated in paprika.

3. Add the tomatoes, red bell pepper and chicken broth and stir to mix everything well.

4. Raise the heat to bring the chicken broth to a boil quickly and then reduce the heat and allow everything to simmer for about 15 minutes.

5. In the meantime, place the chicken thighs on a clean work surface and pound them with a meat tenderizer or rolling pin until they're about 1/2 inch thick.

6. Heat the remaining 1 tablespoon olive oil in a large pan over medium-high heat and sauté the chicken thighs for 5 to 7 minutes on each side, or until golden and firm to the touch. Remove the chicken thighs from the pan and shred them with two forks.

7. Trim the ends off the yellow squash. With the spiralizer on setting 2, spiralize them into thick noodles.

8. Add the shredded chicken, milk, squash noodles and more salt and pepper (if necessary) to the sauce and cook for another 5 minutes. Serve.

**EAT WELL** *with Ming*

DID YOU KNOW PAPRIKA CAN BE USED AS A NATURAL DYE OR FOOD COLORING? IT S A SPICY, BOLD FLAVOR THAT PACKS A DELICIOUS AND TASTY PUNCH!

# Yellow Squash
# BEEF BOLOGNESE

YELLOW SQUASH NOODLES ARE SO MOIST that they can easily pass for traditional pasta in taste and texture. Pair them with a flavorful sauce.

2 TABLESPOONS OLIVE OIL

1 POUND 85% LEAN GROUND BEEF

4 CLOVES GARLIC, MINCED

1 TEASPOON DRIED OREGANO

1 TEASPOON RED PEPPER FLAKES

1 CUP DRY RED WINE

4 ROMA TOMATOES, DICED

SALT AND PEPPER

2 LARGE YELLOW SQUASH

1 TEASPOON DRIED BASIL

1/4 CUP HEAVY CREAM

1/2 CUP GRATED PARMESAN CHEESE

CHOPPED FRESH BASIL, FOR GARNISH

1. Heat the olive oil in a large skillet over medium heat, add the ground beef and sauté for 5 to 7 minutes, until it starts to brown.

2. Add the minced garlic, dried oregano and red pepper flakes and cook for another 2 minutes.

3. Add the wine, tomatoes and salt and pepper to taste and stir well.

4. Bring the sauce to a boil, then lower to a simmer for 10 minutes.

5. Meanwhile, trim the ends off the squash. With the spiralizer on setting 3, spiralize them into thick noodles.

6. Add the dried basil and heavy cream to the sauce, stir and allow to simmer for an additional 10 minutes.

7. In the last 3 minutes, add the yellow squash noodles and cook until soft.

8. Divide the squash and sauce into equal portions, top with the grated Parmesan and fresh basil and serve.

## EAT WELL *with Ming*

DID YOU KNOW THE COMPOUND CAPSAICIN FOUND IN RED PEPPER FLAKES IS KNOWN TO HAVE ANTI-INFLAMMATORY PROPERTIES?

# *Beef* LO MEIN

YOU CAN MAKE A MEATY YET VEGETABLE-PACKED MEAL with eight ingredients and one pan. Enjoy flavor and nutrition with minimal cleanup!

1 TABLESPOON SESAME OIL, OR MORE AS NEEDED

1 POUND FLANK STEAK

8 OUNCES MUSHROOMS, SLICED

1 RED BELL PEPPER, DICED

1 MEDIUM CARROT

2 YELLOW SQUASH

2 TABLESPOONS SOY SAUCE

1 CUP WHOLE SNAP PEAS

SALT AND PEPPER

1. Heat the sesame oil in a very large pan over high heat, add the flank steak and cook for about 5 minutes on each side. Let it rest on a plate for 10 minutes before slicing it.

2. In the leftover sesame oil, cook the mushrooms and diced red bell pepper until slightly browned. Add a bit more sesame oil if necessary.

3. Trim the ends off the carrot and yellow squash and peel the carrot. With the spiralizer on setting 4, spiralize the carrot and the squash into thin noodles and add them to the pan. Toss the noodles to coat them well.

4. Add the soy sauce to the pan and let the noodles cook for about 3 minutes.

5. Slice the flank steak into thin strips and add it to the pan.

6. Add the snap peas and season everything with salt and pepper. Let the flank steak and snap peas cook for about 2 minutes just to warm up.

7. Mix everything well with tongs and divide into equal portions.

## EAT WELL *with Ming*

SNAP PEAS ARE VERY LOW IN CALORIES (UNDER 30 FOR 1 CUP) AND PROVIDE THE PERFECT CRUNCH TO THIS BEEF LO MEIN! USE THEM IN DISHES LIKE THIS FOR A TEXTURAL CONTRAST, AND ENJOY WITH HUMMUS OR DIPS INSTEAD OF CHIPS.

# BEEF STROGANOFF
## with Yellow Squash Ribbons

YOU CAN TURN A CLASSIC CREAMY FAVORITE into a low-carb dish. Yellow squash noodles are the secret ingredient, paired with juicy steak and mushrooms.

1 POUND BEEF TOP SIRLOIN

2 TABLESPOONS OLIVE OIL

2 TABLESPOONS BUTTER

1 POUND MUSHROOMS, SLICED

½ MEDIUM WHITE ONION, DICED

4 CLOVES GARLIC, MINCED

1 CUP BEEF BROTH, LOW SODIUM

2 LARGE YELLOW SQUASH

¼ FULL-FAT GREEK YOGURT

SALT AND PEPPER

FRESH PARSLEY, FOR GARNISH

1. Cut the sirloin steak into thin tips about 1 inch long and ½ inch thick.

2. Heat the olive oil in a large skillet over high heat, add the sirloin tips and brown on both sides, about 5 to 8 minutes. Remove the steak from the pan and place on a plate.

3. Decrease the heat to medium and add the butter and sliced mushrooms to the pan. Scrape up any bits of steak that may be stuck to the skillet with a wooden spoon.

4. After 5 minutes, you should see the mushrooms shrivel a bit and brown. Add the onion and garlic to the pan and cook until the onion turns translucent, about 5 minutes.

5. Pour in the beef broth and add the steak back to the pan. Cover the pan and let everything simmer for about 30 minutes over low heat.

6. Trim the ends off the yellow squash. With the spiralizer on setting 1, spiralize them into ribbons and add the noodles along with the yogurt to the pan. Cook, uncovered, for an additional 10 minutes.

**7.** Season with salt and pepper to taste and stir everything one last time.

**8.** Divide stroganoff into equal portions and garnish with the fresh parsley.

## EAT WELL *with Ming*

USING LOW-SODIUM BEEF BROTH CAN HELP YOU CONTROL YOUR SEASONING AND DECREASE YOUR SODIUM INTAKE.

# THAI SPICY BEEF
## with Cashews

STIR-FRIES OFFER SO MANY QUICK, healthy choices. What you'll especially love about this one: the combination of creamy, spicy and crunchy.

2 MEDIUM ZUCCHINI

2 MEDIUM CARROTS

2 TABLESPOONS OLIVE OIL

1 TABLESPOON LIME JUICE

1/2 RED ONION, DICED

2 CLOVES GARLIC, MINCED

1-INCH CUBE FRESH GINGER, GRATED

1 FRESH JALAPEÑO, SLICED (OPTIONAL)

1 TEASPOON RED PEPPER FLAKES (OPTIONAL)

SALT AND PEPPER

20 OUNCES SIRLOIN STEAK

1/4 CUP LOW-SODIUM BEEF BROTH

2 TABLESPOONS COCONUT MILK

3 OUNCES ROASTED CASHEWS, WHOLE OR CHOPPED

SCALLIONS, CHOPPED, FOR GARNISH

1. Trim the ends off the zucchini and carrots and peel the carrots. With the spiralizer on setting 3, spiralize both the carrots and the zucchini into thick noodles.

2. Add 1 tablespoon of the olive oil and the lime juice to a wok or deep skillet over medium heat and cook the onion, garlic, ginger and carrots for about 5 minutes.

3. Add the zucchini noodles, jalapeño (if using), red pepper flakes (if using) and salt and pepper to taste and cook for 2 more minutes. Set everything aside on a plate while you prepare the rest of the recipe.

4. Slice the sirloin steak into strips about 1/2 inch thick and 1 inch wide. Add them to the same skillet along with the remaining 1 tablespoon of olive oil and cook over medium heat until browned on all sides, about 5 minutes.

5. Add the veggies back to the pan and toss everything well to combine.

6. Pour in the beef broth and coconut milk and allow everything to cook, uncovered, for about 8 minutes. Much of the liquid should be evaporated.

7. Divide the beef and noodles into equal portions and sprinkle with the roasted cashews and chopped scallion. Serve.

**EAT WELL** *with Ming*

CASHEWS, THOUGH HIGHER IN FAT THAN OTHER NUTS, ARE ALSO INCREDIBLY HIGH IN COPPER, A MINERAL ESSENTIAL FOR IRON ABSORPTION.

# BEEF STEW
## *with Butternut Squash*

WHO CAN RESIST STEW IN COOLER MONTHS? This savory combination of hearty beef and sweet butternut squash will satisfy your cravings for comfort food.

3 TABLESPOONS OLIVE OIL

1 MEDIUM YELLOW ONION, CHOPPED

4 CLOVES GARLIC, CHOPPED

2 POUNDS BEEF SIRLOIN STEAK

SALT AND PEPPER

1 CUP DRY RED WINE (WE USE A CABERNET SAUVIGNON)

1 LARGE BUTTERNUT SQUASH

2 ROMA TOMATOES, CHOPPED

1 SPRIG FRESH ROSEMARY

2 CUPS LOW-SODIUM BEEF BROTH

2 CUPS WATER

CHOPPED FRESH PARSLEY, FOR GARNISH

1. Heat the olive oil in a large soup pot over medium heat. Add the onion and garlic and cook until the onion is translucent, about 5 minutes.

2. Cut the beef into 2-inch cubes and season them liberally with salt. Add the cubes to the pot and cook them for about 5 minutes, or until they are brown on all sides.

3. Add the red wine to the pot and stir all the contents with a wooden spoon, gently scraping the bottom to get off all of the caramelized bits.

4. Cut off the bulbous half of the butternut squash. Cut the end of the straighter half off and peel its hard skin multiple times until you reach the bright orange inside. With the spiralizer on setting 1, spiralize the squash into ribbons.

5. Add the butternut ribbons, chopped tomatoes, rosemary, beef broth and water to the pot. Season with salt and pepper to taste.

6. Bring the stew to a boil over high heat and then decrease the heat to low. Cover the pot and let it simmer for 2 to 3 hours. The beef should be fork tender and falling apart easily.

7. Garnish with the chopped fresh parsley and serve.

**EAT WELL** *with Ming*

BUTTERNUT SQUASH IS HIGH IN VITAMIN A, WHICH IS CRITICAL FOR VISION HEALTH, CELL FUNCTION AND IMMUNE SYSTEM FUNCTION.

# CHIMICHURRI SKIRT STEAK *with Broccoli Slaw*

THE BOLD, FRESH FLAVORS OF THE CILANTRO AND GARLIC in the chimichurri (a traditional Argentinean sauce or marinade) pair perfectly with skirt steak. Broccoli slaw complements as a side—in fact, some chimichurris incorporate broccoli right into the sauce.

**SAUCE**

1/2 CUP FINELY MINCED FRESH CILANTRO

1/4 CUP FINELY MINCED FRESH PARSLEY

4 CLOVES GARLIC, SLICED

1 SHALLOT, MINCED

2 TABLESPOONS WHITE VINEGAR

3/4 CUP OLIVE OIL

1 TEASPOON SEA SALT

**STEAK**

1 POUND SKIRT STEAK

1 TEASPOON SEA SALT

1/2 TEASPOON PEPPER

1/2 TEASPOON GARLIC POWDER

1 TABLESPOON OLIVE OIL

**BROCCOLI SLAW**

2 BROCCOLI STEMS

1 MEDIUM CARROT

1/2 HEAD OF WHITE CABBAGE

1/2 CUP MAYONNAISE

JUICE OF 1/2 LEMON

SALT AND PEPPER

1. To make the sauce, combine all the sauce ingredients in a bowl and stir well. Chill it in the fridge until ready to serve.

2. To make the steak, season the skirt steak with the salt, pepper and garlic powder. Heat the olive oil in a pan over high heat, let the pan get very hot, add the steak and cook it for 6 minutes on each side until it's just slightly pink in the center when cut.

Let the steak rest on a plate for 10 minutes before cutting it.

3. To make the broccoli slaw, trim the ends off the broccoli stems and carrots and peel them. With the spiralizer on setting 1, spiralize them both into ribbons. With the spiralizer on setting 1, shred the cabbage.

4. Add all the vegetables to a deep mixing bowl and dress with the

mayonnaise, lemon juice, salt and pepper.

5. Slice the skirt steak into ½- to 1-inch-thick pieces and serve them on top of a bed of the broccoli slaw.

6. Generously dollop each serving with the chilled chimichurri sauce and serve.

# STEAK NOODLE BOWL
## with Thai Peanut Sauce

WARM PEANUT BUTTER is many a chef's secret ingredient. You'll love the rich, creamy texture it adds to the Thai sauce for this Steak Noodle Bowl.

---

### STEAK

1 TABLESPOON OLIVE OIL

24 OUNCES SKIRT STEAK

SALT AND PEPPER

CHOPPED FRESH CILANTRO, FOR GARNISH

WHOLE OR CHOPPED PEANUTS, FOR GARNISH

### PEANUT SAUCE

¼ CUP PEANUT BUTTER

2 TABLESPOONS SOY SAUCE

2 CLOVES GARLIC, MINCED

2 TABLESPOONS LIME JUICE

½-INCH CUBE GINGER

### CARROT NOODLES

4 MEDIUM CARROTS

2 TABLESPOONS OLIVE OIL

½ MEDIUM RED ONION, SLICED

¼ CUP WATER

---

1.  Season the skirt steak liberally with salt and pepper on each side 1 hour before cooking.

2.  Heat a large skillet over medium-high heat with the olive oil, add the steak and cook for 6 to 8 minutes on each side or until it's browned and slightly pink in the center when cut. Remove it from the pan and let it rest on a plate for about 5 minutes before slicing it.

3.  To make the sauce, add the peanut butter to a small pan over medium heat and cook for 3 to 5 minutes, or until the peanut butter melts.

4.  In the meantime, puree the rest of the sauce ingredients in a food processor or blender.

5.  Add the pureed ingredients to the pan with the melted peanut butter and mix everything together well. Remove the pan from the heat.

6. To make the carrot noodles, trim the ends off the carrots and peel them. With the spiralizer on setting 4, spiralize them into thin noodles.

7. Heat the olive oil in a large pan over medium-high heat. Add the sliced onion and cook for about 3 minutes, until the onion starts to soften.

8. Add the carrots and water and cover the pan. Let it steam for about 3 minutes.

9. Slice the steak into thin slices and add them to the pan with the onion and carrots.

10. Pour the peanut sauce into the pan and mix everything together.

11. Divide the steak and noodles among 4 plates, garnish with the cilantro and peanuts and serve.

## EAT WELL with Ming

DID YOU KNOW JUST 1 CUP OF FRESH ONION CONTAINS 20% OF YOUR DAILY VITAMIN $B_6$ TARGET? VITAMIN $B_6$ IS A WATER-SOLUBLE VITAMIN THAT ASSISTS IN MORE THAN 100 DIFFERENT REACTIONS!

# *Steak Fajita* ZOODLES

ZUCCHINI NOODLES can bring satisfying flavor and texture to so many dishes! Pair them with juicy steak and sautéed vegetables.

---

1 POUND SKIRT STEAK

SALT AND PEPPER

1 TABLESPOON OLIVE OIL

1 WHITE ONION, ROUGHLY CHOPPED

1 RED BELL PEPPER, SLICED

1 YELLOW BELL PEPPER, SLICED

2 LARGE ZUCCHINI

1/2 CUP SHREDDED PEPPER JACK CHEESE

JUICE OF 1 LIME

SRIRACHA OR TABASCO SAUCE (OPTIONAL)

CHOPPED FRESH CILANTRO, FOR GARNISH

1. Season the skirt steak liberally with salt and pepper on both sides.

2. Heat the olive oil in a pan over high heat, add the steak and cook for 6 to 8 minutes on each side or until browned and slightly pink in the center. Remove the steak from the pan and let it rest on a plate for 10 minutes before slicing it.

3. In the same pan, cook the chopped onion until it is translucent, about 5 minutes.

4. Add the sliced red and yellow bell peppers, cover the pan and cook them for about 5 minutes, or until softened.

5. Meanwhile, trim the ends off the zucchini. With the spiralizer on setting 3 or 4, spiralize them into noodles according to your preference.

6. Slice the skirt steak into thin strips and add it and the zoodles to the pan. Season again with salt and pepper to taste and toss everything continuously for about 3 minutes.

7. Divide the Steak Fajita Zoodles into equal portions and squeeze some lime juice onto each serving.

8. Drizzle with the hot sauce, if using, and garnish with the fresh cilantro.

**EAT WELL** *with Ming* ————

**JUST 1 CUP OF CHOPPED PEPPERS CONTAINS MORE THAN 250% OF YOUR DAILY VITAMIN C NEEDS!**

# RAMEN WITH STEAK
## and Daikon Noodles

RAMEN IS SAVORED for its umami flavor that warms you through. Daikon noodles and the delicate flavors of soy sauce and honey lighten the soup, while meaty portobello mushrooms and skirt steak satisfy your appetite.

---

10 OUNCES SKIRT STEAK

2 TABLESPOONS
OLIVE OIL

½ WHITE ONION,
CHOPPED

1 RED BELL PEPPER,
CHOPPED

2 CLOVES GARLIC,
MINCED

1 QUART CHICKEN BROTH

2 PORTOBELLO
MUSHROOM CAPS

¼ CUP SOY SAUCE

2 TABLESPOONS HONEY

4 LARGE EGGS

1 DAIKON RADISH

SALT AND PEPPER

JUICE OF 1 LEMON

1. Heat 1 tablespoon of the oil in a skillet, let the pan get very hot, add the steak and sear it for about 1 minute on each side. Remove the steak from the pan and let it rest on a plate before slicing it.

2. Add the remaining 1 tablespoon of oil to a large soup pot over medium heat, add the chopped onion and red bell pepper and cook until the onion is translucent, about 5 minutes.

3. Add the minced garlic and cook for an additional 5 minutes.

4. Pour in the chicken broth and bring the soup to a boil.

5. Slice the portobello mushroom caps into ½-inch-thick pieces and add them to the boiling soup.

6. Lower the heat to a simmer and add the soy sauce and honey.

7. Add the 4 whole eggs (in their shells) and let them cook for 8 minutes, then remove them from the hot soup with tongs and let them cool down.

8. Trim the ends off the daikon radish and peel the outer skin. With the spiralizer on setting 4, spiralize it into thin noodles and add it to the simmering soup.

9. Slice the skirt steak into ½-inch-thick pieces and add them to the soup.

10. Season the soup with salt and pepper and let it simmer for about 10 minutes.

11. Divide the soup into equal servings and add a squeeze of lemon juice to each bowl.

12. Peel the eggs and slice them in half lengthwise. Add 2 egg halves to each bowl and serve.

**EAT WELL** *with Ming*

DID YOU KNOW PORTOBELLO MUSHROOMS ARE A GREAT NONDAIRY SOURCE OF VITAMIN D? JUST 1 PORTOBELLO MUSHROOM CONTAINS MORE THAN 50% OF YOUR DAILY TARGET!

# BALSAMIC THYME STEAK
## on Spinach Parsnip Noodles

A GOOD SALTING CAN GO A LONG WAY to season steak, but if you're ready for a new flavor adventure, try balsamic vinegar and fresh thyme! This steak seasoning combo pairs well with a slightly sweet bed of spinach parsnip noodles.

**STEAK**

24 OUNCES FLANK STEAK

1/4 CUP BALSAMIC VINEGAR

1/4 CUP OLIVE OIL

10 SPRIGS FRESH THYME

1 TEASPOON SALT

1/2 TEASPOON PEPPER

**NOODLES**

1 TABLESPOON OLIVE OIL

12 OUNCES SPINACH

2 LARGE PARSNIPS

SALT AND PEPPER

1. To make the steak, marinate the flank steak ahead of time to ensure a softer, juicier result. Whisk together the balsamic vinegar, olive oil, fresh thyme sprigs, salt and pepper in a baking dish. Submerge the flank steak entirely and let it sit in the refrigerator overnight, or for at least 4 hours.

2. When ready to cook, preheat the oven to the broil setting with a 12-inch cast-iron skillet or other large oven-safe pan inside.

3. After about 10 minutes, take the cast-iron skillet out of the oven with an oven mitt and place it on the stove.

4. Sear the flank steak on each side for about 30 seconds. The heat from the cast-iron skillet should be enough to sear it without turning on the burner.

5. Transfer the skillet back to the oven and broil for about 5 minutes on each side until sizzling and browned. Be sure to use an oven mitt each time. Remove it from the oven and let it rest, covered, for about 10 minutes.

6. To make the noodles, heat the olive oil in a large frying pan over medium heat, add the spinach and let it wilt.

7. Trim the ends off the parsnips and peel them. With the spiralizer on setting 1, spiralize them into thin noodles and add them to the pan. Toss the parsnip noodles to coat them in the olive oil and wilted spinach. Season with salt and pepper.

8. Lower the heat, cover the noodles and let them cook for about 8 minutes, or until softened.

9. Slice the steak against the grain of the meat into thin slices.

10. Divide the noodles into equal portions and top with the sliced flank steak.

EAT WELL *with Ming*

FLANK STEAK IS A GREAT CHOICE IF YOU ARE IN THE MOOD FOR RED MEAT. IT S ONE OF THE LEANEST CUTS. PAIRED WITH THE SPINACH PARSNIP NOODLES, IT MAKES THE PERFECT HEARTY MEAL!

# *Thai Beef* DRUNKEN NOODLES

THE TRADITIONAL NAME for Drunken Noodles is Pad Kee Mao. Whatever you call them, they're a simple, flavorful dinner. In this version you get sweet, savory, spicy and salty all in one dish, with added nutrition from subbing in parsnip noodles!

---

2 LARGE PARSNIPS

1 OUNCE FRESH THAI BASIL, PLUS MORE FOR GARNISH

1 TABLESPOON SESAME OR OLIVE OIL

12 OUNCES SIRLOIN STEAK

1/2 WHITE ONION, CHOPPED

4 CLOVES GARLIC, CHOPPED

1-INCH CUBE GINGER, GRATED

2 MEDIUM CARROTS

1 MEDIUM ZUCCHINI

2 TABLESPOONS SOY SAUCE

SALT AND BLACK PEPPER

2 SCALLIONS, CHOPPED

1/2 TEASPOON RED PEPPER FLAKES (OPTIONAL)

---

1. Bring a pot of lightly salted water to a boil over medium-high heat.

2. Trim the ends off the parsnips and peel them. With the spiralizer on setting 2, spiralize them into thick noodles. Add the noodles to the boiling water and cook for 5 to 6 minutes, or until soft.

3. Drain the water and add the basil to the hot noodles. Stir the leaves in and allow them to wilt in the parsnips' residual heat.

4. Heat the sesame oil in a skillet or wok over high heat, add the sirloin steak and cook for 4 to 6 minutes on each side, depending on the thickness of the steak. The steak should be brown and slightly pink in the center when cut. Remove the steak from the pan and let it rest on a plate before slicing it.

5. Lower the heat, add the white onion to the pan and cook until translucent, about 5 minutes. Add the chopped garlic and grated ginger and cook until fragrant, about 3 minutes.

6. Chop the carrots into ¼-inch-thick rounds, add them to the pan and cook them until they're a bit soft, about 5 to 6 minutes.

7. Slice the zucchini into thick sticks, add them to the pan and cook until they are soft and slightly browned, about 4 to 5 minutes.

8. Slice the cooked steak and add it back to the pan with the soy sauce. Season with salt and pepper and toss to combine. Cook about a minute.

9. Add the parsnip noodles and toss to combine. Divide the mixture among 4 plates and top with more fresh basil, chopped scallion and red pepper flakes, if using.

**EAT WELL** *with Ming* ——————————

USING SPIRALIZED PARSNIPS INSTEAD OF NOODLES HELPS DECREASE CALORIES AND INCREASE NUTRIENTS AND FIBER IN THIS DRUNKEN NOODLE DISH. PAIRED WITH THE INCREDIBLE THAI BASIL, IT'S SUCH A DELICIOUS DISH, YOU'LL NEVER KNOW THE DIFFERENCE!

# GRILLED SAUSAGE
## with Butternut Squash Noodles

SAUSAGES HOT OFF THE GRILL are a summertime favorite. But you can dress up the dinner with a very simple addition: honey-glazed butternut squash noodles. It's a great combo everyone will rave over.

| | | |
|---|---|---|
| 1 LARGE BUTTERNUT SQUASH | 2 TABLESPOONS OLIVE OIL | 4 OUNCES FRESH KALE |
| | | SALT |
| 12 (1-OUNCE) PORK SAUSAGE LINKS, COOKED | 1 SMALL WHITE ONION, DICED | 2 TABLESPOONS HONEY |

1. Preheat a grill to about 400°F.

2. Cut off the bulbous half of the butternut squash. Cut the end of the straighter half off and peel its hard skin multiple times until you reach the bright orange inside. With the spiralizer on setting 2 or 3, spiralize the squash into thick noodles.

3. Make a few slices into each sausage link on one side about a quarter of the way in. Grill them for about 10 minutes, flipping them halfway through.

4. Heat the oil in a large pan over medium heat, add the onion and cook until the onion is translucent, about 5 minutes.

5. Add the butternut noodles and kale and cook them for 10 minutes. Season everything with salt to taste.

6. On a serving platter, make a bed out of the butternut noodles, kale and onions and drizzle with the honey. Add the sausage links on top and serve.

## EAT WELL with Ming

KALE IS A NUTRITION POWERHOUSE—IT'S NO WONDER WHY IT'S BEEN ALL THE RAGE LATELY! JUST 1 CUP HAS MORE THAN 100% OF YOUR DAILY VITAMIN A NEEDS AND MORE THAN 1,000% OF YOUR VITAMIN K NEEDS!

# SAUSAGE AND PEPPERS
## *with Zoodles*

THIS ONE-PAN DINNER works for even busy families. When cooked in a sweet marinara sauce with zesty sausage, the zucchini will sneak right by the kids.

---

2 TABLESPOONS
OLIVE OIL

1 WHITE ONION,
ROUGHLY CHOPPED

1 RED BELL PEPPER,
ROUGHLY CHOPPED

1 YELLOW BELL PEPPER,
ROUGHLY CHOPPED

4 CLOVES GARLIC,
ROUGHLY CHOPPED

6 ANDOUILLE SAUSAGES,
COOKED

2 CUPS MARINARA SAUCE
(STORE-BOUGHT OR SEE
RECIPE ON PAGE 11)

2 LARGE ZUCCHINI

SALT AND PEPPER

SHAVED PARMESAN
CHEESE, FOR GARNISH

FRESH BASIL LEAVES,
FOR GARNISH

1. Heat the olive oil in a large pan over medium heat, add the onion and red and yellow peppers and cook for 6 to 8 minutes.

2. Add the chopped garlic and cook everything for about 3 minutes longer, until the garlic is fragrant.

3. Slice the Andouille sausages into ½-inch-thick pieces and add them to the pan. Let the sausages cook for about 5 minutes just to heat them through. Add the marinara sauce, stir with a wooden spoon to combine everything and lower the heat to a simmer.

4. Meanwhile, with the spiralizer on setting 2, 3 or 4, spiralize the zucchini into thin or thick noodles according to your preference.

5. Add the noodles to the pan and make sure they are more or less submerged under the marinara sauce. Let the noodles cook for 3 to 5 minutes until they've softened.

6. Test to see if the dish needs salt and pepper and add as necessary.

7. Divide everything into equal portions and top each plate with shaved (or grated) Parmesan cheese and fresh basil leaves.

**EAT WELL** *with Ming*

JUST 1 CUP OF ZUCCHINI CONTAINS NEARLY ONE-FIFTH OF YOUR DAILY COPPER
NEEDS. COPPER IS AN ESSENTIAL TRACE MINERAL IN ALL OUR TISSUES AND AIDS
IRON IN RED BLOOD CELL PRODUCTION.

# SPAGHETTI AND MEATBALLS *Marinara*

IT'S ALWAYS A SMART IDEA to take a traditional pasta dish and sub in spiralized vegetables. Spaghetti is a great place to start—especially for kids.

1 POUND 85% LEAN GROUND BEEF

1 TEASPOON DRIED OREGANO

1 TEASPOON DRIED BASIL

SALT AND PEPPER

1 TABLESPOON OLIVE OIL

2 CLOVES GARLIC, MINCED

2 CUPS MARINARA SAUCE (STORE-BOUGHT OR SEE RECIPE ON PAGE 11)

2 MEDIUM YELLOW SQUASH

CHOPPED FRESH BASIL, FOR GARNISH

1. Place the ground beef in a bowl, add the oregano and dried basil and season with salt and pepper. Using your hands, combine the mixture well.

2. Shape the ground beef into ½-inch meatballs. You should be able to make about 30 small meatballs.

3. Heat the olive oil in a large pan over high heat and sear the meatballs for about 5 minutes total. Rotate them every now and then to ensure even cooking.

4. Reduce the heat to medium-low. Add the garlic and marinara sauce to the meatballs. Cover the pan and let it all simmer for about 15 minutes.

5. Trim the ends off the yellow squash. With the spiralizer on setting 3, spiralize them into thick noodles.

6. When there is 3 minutes of cooking time left, add the noodles to the pan and mix them into the sauce well.

7. Garnish with the fresh basil and serve.

## EAT WELL *with Ming*

MAKING MEATBALLS WITH A FATTIER CUT OF MEAT WILL HELP THEM STAY TOGETHER WHILE COOKING. ADDITIONALLY, BY MAKING MEATBALLS, YOU ARE CREATING PERFECT LITTLE PORTIONS TO HELP WITH PORTION CONTROL!

# PORK AND PINEAPPLE KEBABS *with Marinated Squash*

**WHICH IS THE MAIN, AND WHICH IS THE SIDE?** This pairing works together with bold flavors that complement and satisfy. It's a complete, delicious dinner experience.

---

SQUASH AND MARINADE
1 MEDIUM EGGPLANT

SALT AND PEPPER

2 TABLESPOONS
WHITE VINEGAR

2 TABLESPOONS
LEMON JUICE

2 CLOVES GARLIC,
MINCED

1/3 CUP OLIVE OIL

2 MEDIUM ZUCCHINI

2 MEDIUM YELLOW
SQUASH

KEBABS
1 POUND PORK
TENDERLOIN, CUBED

2 TABLESPOONS
LEMON JUICE

2 TABLESPOONS
SOY SAUCE

SALT AND PEPPER

8 OUNCES PINEAPPLE,
CUBED

2 FRESH JALAPEÑO
PEPPERS, CUT INTO
CHUNKS

1. If you're using wooden skewers, be sure to soak them in water to prevent them from burning on the grill.

2. To make the squash and marinade, cut the eggplant into 1-inch cubes and place them in a colander. Liberally salt the eggplant cubes and let them sit for about 30 minutes, then rinse them and pat them dry with a clean kitchen towel or paper towels.

3. Add the vinegar, lemon juice, garlic and salt and pepper to taste to a medium mixing bowl and whisk to mix everything together. Gradually whisk in the oil a little at a time until the mixture is emulsified.

4. Trim the ends off the zucchini and yellow squash. With the spiralizer on setting 2 or 3, spiralize them into thick noodles.

5. Transfer the noodles and eggplant cubes to a large bowl and add half the marinade. Allow this to marinate for at least 2 hours.

6. To make the kebabs, add the pork cubes, lemon juice, soy sauce and salt and pepper to taste to a mixing bowl and toss well.

7. Preheat the grill to medium-high heat (400°F to 450°F) and preheat the oven to 350°F.

8. Thread the pork, pineapple and jalapeño chunks alternately onto wooden skewers.

9. Grill each skewer for about 7 minutes on each side.

10. Transfer the eggplant and noodles to a baking dish and bake them for 10 to 15 minutes, tossing them gently if needed.

11. Place the skewers on a plate with the marinated noodles on the side. Drizzle the noodles with the remaining half of the marinade and serve.

**EAT WELL** *with Ming* ───

PINEAPPLE NOT ONLY ADDS THE PERFECT SWEET FLAVOR TO THIS DISH, BUT IT ALSO PACKS A CITRUS AND VITAMIN C PUNCH. JUST 1 CUP CONTAINS MORE THAN 100% OF YOUR DAILY VITAMIN C TARGET!

# SESAME PORK ZUCCHINI *Stir-Fry*

IN ABOUT 20 MINUTES, you can create a flavorful stir-fry filled with garden vegetables. The seasonings are so simple you probably have them on hand!

24 OUNCES BONELESS PORK LOIN

2 TABLESPOONS OLIVE OIL

½ MEDIUM WHITE ONION, CHOPPED

8 OUNCES WHITE MUSHROOMS, SLICED

2 TABLESPOONS SOY SAUCE

4 CUPS BROCCOLI FLORETS

1 CUP WHOLE SNAP PEAS

2 CLOVES GARLIC, DICED

SALT AND PEPPER

2 LARGE ZUCCHINI

1 TABLESPOON SESAME OIL

2 TEASPOONS TOASTED SESAME SEEDS

1. Slice the pork into ½-inch-thick slices.

2. Heat the olive oil in a deep skillet or wok over medium heat, add the pork and cook for 5 minutes.

3. Add the chopped onion and mushrooms to the pan and cook for 5 to 7 minutes, until the onion becomes translucent.

4. Add the soy sauce, broccoli, snap peas, garlic and salt and pepper to taste and continue to cook for 5 minutes, stirring continuously.

5. Trim the ends off the zucchini. With the spiralizer on setting 3, spiralize them into thick noodles. Add them to the pan along with the sesame oil. Let everything cook for 2 more minutes.

6. Garnish with the sesame seeds and serve.

**EAT WELL** *with Ming*

LOADED WITH VITAMINS C AND K AND FOLATE, BROCCOLI IS A COMPLETE SUPERSTAR WHEN IT COMES TO PACKING IN NUTRIENTS!

# SOY-GLAZED SALMON
## with Broccoli and Carrot Noodles

A SLIGHTLY SPICY SOY SAUCE infuses these salmon fillets with flavor and moisture. Broccoli and carrot noodles add hearty texture and nutrition.

---

1 FRESH JALAPEÑO, MINCED

1 BUNCH SCALLIONS, CHOPPED

1/2 CUP SOY SAUCE

JUICE OF 1 LEMON

4 (6-OUNCE) SALMON FILLETS

4 BROCCOLI STEMS

2 LARGE CARROTS

2 TABLESPOONS OLIVE OIL

SALT AND PEPPER

1. Combine the jalapeño, scallions, soy sauce and lemon juice in a large bowl. Stir to combine and add the salmon fillets. Cover the bowl with plastic wrap and allow the salmon to marinate for at least 30 minutes in the refrigerator.

2. In the meantime, trim the ends off the broccoli stems and carrots and peel both veggies. With the spiralizer on setting 3, spiralize them both into thick noodles.

3. Heat 1 tablespoon of the olive oil in a skillet over medium heat, add the noodles and cook for about 5 minutes or until slightly softened. Season the noodles with salt and pepper to taste.

4. Heat the remaining 1 tablespoon of oil in another pan over medium heat, add the salmon fillets and cook for 5 to 7 minutes on each side. The salmon should flake easily with a fork.

5. Make a bed of broccoli and carrot noodles on each of 4 plates and place a salmon fillet on top, or shred the salmon and toss everything together.

## EAT WELL with Ming

DID YOU KNOW JALAPEÑOS ARE MORE THAN JUST SPICY PEPPERS? JUST 1 JALAPEÑO CONTAINS MORE THAN 100% OF YOUR DAILY VITAMIN C TARGET!

# CILANTRO LIME SALMON
## with Broccoli and Carrot Noodles

CITRUS BRINGS OUT THE MILD FLAVOR of seafood, but don't get stuck in a lemon rut. Lime can work just as well, as in this Cilantro Lime Salmon recipe.

1 CUP CHOPPED FRESH CILANTRO

2 CLOVES GARLIC

JUICE OF 1 LIME

3 TABLESPOONS OLIVE OIL

4 (6-OUNCE) SALMON FILLETS

SALT AND PEPPER

4 BROCCOLI STEMS

2 MEDIUM CARROTS

1. Preheat the oven to 400°F. Line a 13 x 9-inch baking sheet with foil.

2. Using a food processor or blender, puree the cilantro, garlic, lime juice and 1 tablespoon of the olive oil together.

3. Spread 1 tablespoon of olive oil evenly on the prepared baking sheet and place the salmon fillets, skin side down, on top.

4. Season the salmon with salt and pepper and spread the cilantro lime sauce over the top. Bake for 10 to 15 minutes or until it is easily flaked with a fork.

5. In the meantime, trim the ends of the broccoli stems and carrots and peel them. With the spiralizer on setting 3, spiralize them into thick noodles.

6. Heat the remaining 1 tablespoon of oil in a large pan over medium heat, add the noodles and cook for 3 to 5 minutes, tossing continuously, until they've slightly softened. Season with salt and pepper to taste.

7. Serve the salmon on a bed of broccoli and carrot noodles with any of the remaining cilantro lime sauce from the pan

## EAT WELL with Ming

SALMON IS MORE THAN JUST A DELICIOUS AND VERSATILE FISH. IT CONTAINS MORE THAN 100% OF YOUR SELENIUM NEEDS IN ONE 4-OUNCE SERVING.

# TUNA TARTARE *Noodle Bowl*

DON'T MISS OUT ON FLAVOR because you're hesitant to work with raw fish! Just purchase sushi-grade tuna and prep the fish quickly. The silky texture of the tuna and avocado pair well with the crunch of the cucumber noodles and sesame seeds.

---

**24 OUNCES SUSHI-GRADE TUNA**

**1 LARGE AVOCADO, PITTED AND PEELED**

**¼ CUP MAYONNAISE**

**2 TABLESPOONS SOY SAUCE**

**1 TEASPOON DIJON MUSTARD**

**2 TEASPOONS SRIRACHA SAUCE (OPTIONAL)**

**1 CUCUMBER**

**SALT AND PEPPER**

**SESAME SEEDS, FOR GARNISH**

1. Dice the fresh tuna and avocado into small cubes and add them to a mixing bowl.

2. Combine the mayonnaise, soy sauce, mustard and sriracha, if using, in a small bowl, pour over the tuna and avocado and mix them gently.

3. Trim the ends off the cucumber and peel it. With the spiralizer on setting 3, spiralize it into thick noodles and add it to the mixing bowl. Season with salt and pepper to taste and toss all the ingredients well.

4. Garnish each serving with sesame seeds.

## EAT WELL *with Ming*

TUNA IS A VERY VERSATILE FISH THAT IS HIGH IN OMEGA-3 FATTY ACIDS, WHICH HELP DECREASE INFLAMMATION AND PROTECT AGAINST HEART DISEASE.

# PARMESAN-CRUSTED COD
## with Broccoli Noodles

PARMESAN CHEESE just makes everything more flavorful—it's an easy upgrade from the usual bread crumbs and crisps beautifully in the oven. Broccoli noodles cook in just minutes for a simple, nutritious accent.

---

1 LARGE EGG

1/3 CUP GRATED
PARMESAN CHEESE

1 TEASPOON
GARLIC POWDER

SALT AND PEPPER

4 (6-OUNCE)
COD FILLETS

4 BROCCOLI STEMS

2 TABLESPOONS
OLIVE OIL

SHAVED PARMESAN,
FOR GARNISH

1. Preheat the oven to 450°F. Line a 13 x 9-inch baking sheet with foil and grease the foil.

2. Beat the egg in a wide bowl.

3. In another bowl, mix the Parmesan cheese with the garlic powder and salt and pepper to taste and spread the mixture out evenly on a large, shallow plate.

4. Dredge the cod fillets evenly in the egg and then gently press each one in the Parmesan cheese mixture until they're all fully coated.

5. Arrange the fillets carefully in the prepared baking dish, making sure each has room and they aren't touching.

6. Bake the fillets for 10 to 15 minutes, or until they turn golden brown.

7. Meanwhile, trim the ends of the broccoli stems and peel them. With the spiralizer on setting 3, spiralize them into thick noodles.

8. Heat the oil in a skillet over medium heat, add the broccoli noodles and cook for 2 to 3 minutes, tossing continuously until they've slightly softened.

9. Make a bed of the cooked broccoli noodles on each of 4 plates, place a cod fillet on top and garnish with the shaved Parmesan cheese to serve.

**EAT WELL** *with Ming*

COD IS ANOTHER EXTREMELY VERSATILE FISH AND A GREAT SOURCE OF SELENIUM. THIS TRACE ELEMENT IS NOT ONLY NUTRITIONALLY ESSENTIAL, BUT IT ALSO CONTRIBUTES TO MORE THAN TWO DOZEN DIFFERENT PROTEINS!

# MARINARA SHRIMP
## and Mushroom Zoodles

THIS RECIPE IS THE BEST OF TWO WORLDS of cuisine, featuring both Italian and Asian influences. But it's quick and easy enough to enjoy any night of the week!

1 TABLESPOON OLIVE OIL

8 OUNCES BABY BELLA OR WHITE MUSHROOMS, SLICED

2 CLOVES GARLIC, MINCED

1 POUND LARGE SHRIMP, PEELED AND DEVEINED

1/2 TEASPOON DRIED BASIL

1/2 TEASPOON RED PEPPER FLAKES

SALT AND PEPPER

2 ZUCCHINI

1 CUP MARINARA SAUCE (STORE-BOUGHT OR SEE RECIPE ON PAGE 11)

2 TABLESPOONS GRATED PARMESAN CHEESE

CHOPPED FRESH BASIL, FOR GARNISH

1. Heat the olive oil in a large pan over high heat. Add the sliced mushrooms and let them cook until slightly browned, 5 to 7 minutes.

2. Add the minced garlic to the pan and cook for about 5 minutes longer, or until the garlic is fragrant.

3. Next, add the shrimp and cook for 2 to 3 minutes on each side, or until pink throughout. Season it all with the dried basil, red pepper flakes and salt and pepper to taste.

4. Remove the mixture from the pan, place in a bowl and let it rest while you prepare the noodles.

5. Trim the ends off the zucchini. With the spiralizer on setting 4, spiralize them into thin noodles.

6. Lower the heat, add the marinara sauce to the same pan and allow it to come to a simmer. Add the zoodles and let them cook for about 5 minutes, or until softened, tossing continuously.

7. Add the shrimp mixture back into the pan and toss well to combine.

8. Serve with a sprinkle of grated Parmesan cheese and fresh basil to garnish.

## EAT WELL *with Ming*

SHRIMP IS AN EXCELLENT LOW-CALORIE PROTEIN SOURCE. IT'S ALSO A GREAT SOURCE OF SELENIUM, WHICH IS NEEDED FOR ITS ANTIOXIDANT PROPERTIES IN HELPING PREVENT CELL DAMAGE.

# RAINBOW SHRIMP *Stir-Fry*

SO MANY COLORFUL FRESH VEGETABLES make this stir-fry look as amazing as it tastes. It can brighten up any dinner party or ordinary weeknight dinner.

2 TABLESPOONS OLIVE OIL

½ LARGE RED ONION

2 YELLOW BELL PEPPERS

2 MEDIUM ZUCCHINI

2 MEDIUM CARROTS

SALT AND PEPPER

24 OUNCES LARGE SHRIMP, PEELED AND DEVEINED

1 CUP SHELLED EDAMAME

4 FRESH BASIL LEAVES, CHOPPED

1. Heat the olive oil in a skillet over medium heat. Chop the onion and peppers into thin strips, add them to the pan and cook them until softened, about 5 minutes.

2. Trim the ends off zucchini and the carrots and peel the carrots. With the spiralizer on setting 4, spiralize both vegetables into thin noodles and add them to the pan. Season with salt and pepper to taste and let them cook for 3 minutes, or until softened a bit.

3. Remove the veggies from the pan, place in a bowl and add the shrimp and edamame to the pan. Cook for 3 to 5 minutes, flipping the shrimp, until all the shrimp turn pink.

4. Add the cooked noodles back into the pan and toss everything to combine.

5. Divide into equal portions and garnish with the chopped basil leaves.

## EAT WELL *with Ming*

NOT ONLY DOES THIS DISH HAVE SHRIMP, A GREAT SOURCE OF PROTEIN, BUT IT ALSO HAS EDAMAME, ANOTHER SOURCE OF PROTEIN! EDAMAME ARE PACKED WITH PROTEIN AND FIBER, TWO NUTRIENTS ESSENTIAL FOR KEEPING YOU FULL.

# LEMON GINGER SCALLOPS
## on Roasted Butternut Ribbons

WHEN CITRUSY SCALLOPS MEET SWEET, roasted butternut squash, the taste is heaven. This meal comes together quickly because the squash and scallop cooking times can overlap.

**NOODLES**

2 BUTTERNUT SQUASH

2 TABLESPOONS COCONUT OIL, MELTED

1 TEASPOON SEA SALT

**SCALLOPS**

2 TABLESPOONS OLIVE OIL

JUICE OF 1 LEMON

1-INCH CUBE GINGER, GRATED

SALT AND PEPPER

16 SCALLOPS

LEMON ZEST, FOR GARNISH

1. Preheat the oven to 400°F. Line a 13 x 9-inch baking sheet with foil.

2. To make the noodles, cut off the bulbous half of each butternut squash. Cut the end of the straighter half off and peel its hard skin multiple times until you reach the bright orange inside. With the spiralizer on setting 1, spiralize the butternut squash into ribbons.

3. In a large mixing bowl, toss the butternut squash ribbons in the melted coconut oil and salt and then arrange them evenly on the prepared baking sheet.

4. Bake the butternut squash ribbons for 10 minutes. Turn on the broiler and broil the ribbons for 2 to 3 minutes, or until they've browned slightly.

5. Meanwhile, to make the scallops, in a large bowl, whisk together the olive oil, lemon juice, grated ginger and salt and pepper to taste.

6. Add the scallops to the bowl and toss gently to combine. Let this sit for about 10 minutes.

7. Heat a frying pan over high heat until hot, add the scallops with a bit of their marinade and cook for 4 minutes on each side, or until they are lightly browned on each side.

8. Divide the roasted butternut squash ribbons among 4 plates, top each pile with 4 scallops, sprinkle with lemon zest and serve.

## EAT WELL *with Ming*

SCALLOPS ARE A GOOD SOURCE OF VITAMIN $B_6$, BENEFICIAL FOR YOUR BRAIN. THEY ALSO ARE LOADED WITH PHOSPHORUS, WHICH HELPS WITH BONE AND TEETH HEALTH AND (IN CONJUNCTION WITH OTHER B VITAMINS) IS IMPORTANT FOR KIDNEY FUNCTION, MUSCLE CONTRACTION, HEARTBEAT REGULARITY AND NERVE SIGNALING.

# SCALLOPS AND SPAGHETTI
## with Avocado Lime Sauce

AVOCADO ADDS DELICIOUS CREAMINESS to just about anything, including sauces for spiralized vegetables. Avocado also contains healthy fats, so you can feel good about enjoying this recipe.

2 TABLESPOONS OLIVE OIL

12 SCALLOPS

NOODLES
1 TABLESPOON UNSALTED BUTTER

2 CLOVES GARLIC, MINCED

2 YELLOW SQUASH

AVOCADO LIME SAUCE
1 MEDIUM AVOCADO

JUICE OF 1 LIME

2 TABLESPOONS AVOCADO OIL OR OLIVE OIL

2 TABLESPOONS MAYONNAISE

SALT AND PEPPER

1. Heat the oil in a large skillet over high heat, add the scallops and cook for 4 minutes on each side, or until lightly browned on each side.

2. To make the noodles, melt the butter in another large pan over medium heat, then add the minced garlic to the pan. Let this cook until fragrant, but not brown.

3. Trim the ends off the yellow squash. With the spiralizer on setting 3, spiralize them into thick noodles. Add them to the pan with the garlic and let them cook for about 3 minutes, tossing continuously.

Remove the pan from the heat while you prepare the sauce.

4. To make the sauce, cut open the avocado, remove the pit and scoop the flesh into the bowl of a food processor. Add the lime juice, avocado oil, mayonnaise and salt and pepper to taste to the food processor and blend everything until it reaches a smooth consistency.

5. Make a bed of noodles on each of 4 plates, add a good dollop of the Avocado Lime Sauce and place 3 scallops on top. Serve.

AVOCADOS ARE ABSOLUTELY DELICIOUS WHEN THEY ARE TENDER AND RIPE, AND A GOOD SOURCE OF FIBER AND LINOLEIC ACID. TEST RIPENESS BY CHECKING THE LITTLE NUB AT THE TOP: IF IT FALLS OFF EASILY AND YOU SEE GREEN, IT'S GOOD TO GO!

# *Spinach and Crème Fraîche*
# FRITTATA

FRITTATAS ARE FIT FOR BREAKFAST, lunch or dinner when they contain filling, flavorful vegetables like this recipe with spinach, zucchini and parsnip noodles. If you don't have crème fraîche, you can sub in sour cream.

2 TABLESPOONS
OLIVE OIL

1 WHITE ONION, DICED

24 OUNCES FRESH
SPINACH

2 ZUCCHINI

1 MEDIUM PARSNIP

SALT AND PEPPER

8 LARGE EGGS

6 OUNCES CRÈME
FRAÎCHE OR SOUR CREAM

½ CUP SHREDDED
MOZZARELLA CHEESE

1. Preheat the oven to 350°F.

2. Heat the olive oil in a large oven-safe skillet over medium heat, add the white onion and cook until the onion is translucent, about 5 minutes.

3. Add the fresh spinach to the pan a few handfuls at a time until all of it has wilted.

4. Trim the ends off the zucchini and parsnip and peel the parsnip. With the spiralizer on setting 4, spiralize them both into thin noodles.

5. Add the noodles to the pan and let them cook for about 5 minutes, tossing continuously. Season them with salt and pepper.

6. Meanwhile, crack the eggs into in a mixing bowl and whisk very well. Add the crème fraîche and whisk vigorously to disperse it a bit.

7. Add the whisked eggs to the pan, covering all the spinach and pressing the noodles in so they're completely submerged.

8. Transfer the pan to the hot oven and bake for about 10 minutes, or until the eggs are set.

9. Take the frittata out and add the shredded mozzarella cheese over the whole top. Turn on the broiler and broil the frittata for about 2 minutes, keeping an eye on the cheese so it doesn't burn.

10. Cut the frittata into slices and serve.

## EAT WELL *with Ming*

SPINACH IS ANOTHER NUTRITION SUPERHERO! JUST 3 OUNCES—WHAT YOU'D GET FROM ONE SERVING OF THIS FRITTATA—PROVIDES MORE THAN 35% FOLATE, 400% VITAMIN K, 25% VITAMIN C, 50% VITAMIN A AND 20% MAGNESIUM NEEDS FOR THE DAY.

# CHEESY ZUCCHINI FRITTERS *with Bacon*

LOOKING FOR A NEW AND FUN TASTE? These zucchini fritters feature crispy outsides that are filled with crunchy bacon bits and creamy cheddar cheese.

---

2 TO 3 CUPS AVOCADO OIL

2 ZUCCHINI

2 TABLESPOONS SEA SALT

12 BACON STRIPS, COOKED AND CRUMBLED

6 OUNCES SHREDDED CHEDDAR CHEESE

2 CLOVES GARLIC, MINCED

2 LARGE EGGS

3 TABLESPOONS COCONUT FLOUR

SALT AND PEPPER

CHOPPED PARSLEY, FOR GARNISH

1. Heat the avocado oil in a small pot over high heat while you prepare the recipe. If you don't have avocado oil, use any other mild-tasting oil with a high smoke point, like coconut oil.

2. Trim the ends off the zucchini. With the spiralizer on setting 4, spiralize them into thin noodles. Add them to a strainer set over a large bowl and sprinkle them generously with salt. Let the noodles sit for about 30 minutes so that some of the water can drain from them. Squeeze the noodles gently with a paper towel to get some excess water out. Discard the excess water.

3. Combine the drained noodles with the crumbled bacon and shredded cheddar in a mixing bowl.

4. Add the garlic, eggs and coconut flour to the noodle mixture. If you don't have coconut flour, use your favorite gluten-free flour, though you may need to use a bit more of it. Season with salt and pepper and mix everything very well with your hands.

5. Grab a handful and start shaping the mixture into thin patties 4 to 5 inches in diameter.

6. Test if the oil is ready by either using a thermometer (it should read 350°F) or by dipping a strand of zucchini in. If the oil starts sizzling after more than 2 seconds, it's not ready.

7. When the oil is at the right temperature, gently lower 1 or 2 fritters in at a time and fry them for about 6 minutes. Flip them a few times to ensure one side doesn't get too brown.

8. Serve warm with chopped parsley.

**EAT WELL** *with Ming*

USING COCONUT FLOUR IS AN EXCELLENT WAY TO KEEP THESE FRITTERS GLUTEN FREE SO THAT ALL WITH FOOD ALLERGIES CAN ENJOY THEM!

# *Zucchini Lasagna* ROSETTES

LASAGNA LAYERS can take a ton of time to prep and can add up to a lot of calories. Try this new spin on single-size lasagna portions made with zoodles! You save time and calories but don't need to sacrifice on that cheesy lusciousness you love.

2 LARGE ZUCCHINI

1 CUP WHOLE MILK RICOTTA

6 LARGE EGGS

1/2 TEASPOON SEA SALT

1/4 TEASPOON PEPPER

1/2 TEASPOON DRIED BASIL

1/2 TEASPOON DRIED OREGANO

1/2 CUP SHREDDED MOZZARELLA CHEESE

8 TABLESPOONS TOMATO PASTE

SHAVED OR GRATED PARMESAN CHEESE, FOR GARNISH

1. Preheat the oven to 350°F. Grease 8 cups of a 12-cup muffin tin.

2. Trim the ends off the zucchini. With the spiralizer on setting 1, spiralize them into ribbons.

3. Add a handful of ribbons to each of the prepared muffin cups, reserving some for the top.

4. Scoop the ricotta cheese into the center of a clean kitchen towel or piece of cheesecloth folded a few times, draw the corners of the cloth together, twist the cloth and squeeze some of the excess moisture out of the ricotta cheese. This will make

the end result set much better. We recommend not skipping this step.

5. In a mixing bowl, whisk together the eggs, drained ricotta, salt, pepper, basil and oregano. Pour the mixture over the zucchini ribbons, making sure to get it into all the crevices.

6. Add a bit of the shredded mozzarella cheese to each rosette as well as 1 tablespoon of tomato paste in the center.

7. Add some of the reserved bits of zucchini ribbons to the tops to garnish and make each one look like petals of a flower.

8. Transfer the muffin pan to the oven and bake for 15 minutes. The rosettes should be set on top. Remove the pan from the oven and then let the rosettes cool on a wire rack for about 20 minutes to help them set. Remove the rosettes from the muffin cups.

9. Serve warm with a sprinkle of Parmesan cheese.

## EAT WELL *with Ming*

LASAGNA IS ALWAYS A FAVORITE! USING WHOLE MILK RICOTTA INCREASES CALCIUM, PLUS THE HIGH FAT CONTENT WILL KEEP YOU FULL. THE ROSETTE TECHNIQUE HELPS WITH PORTION CONTROL.

# RATATOUILLE *Casserole*

**WARM LAYERS OF COLORFUL ROASTED VEGETABLES** topped with mozzarella cheese almost make this dish look too good to eat. But you won't be able to resist the aroma coming from your oven!

---

1 CUP MARINARA SAUCE (STORE-BOUGHT OR SEE RECIPE ON PAGE 11)

1 SMALL YELLOW ONION

1 MEDIUM YELLOW SQUASH

1 MEDIUM ZUCCHINI

3 CAMPARI TOMATOES

1 SMALL EGGPLANT

1 TABLESPOON RED WINE VINEGAR

1/2 TEASPOON DRIED BASIL

1/2 TEASPOON DRIED OREGANO

SALT AND PEPPER

4 OUNCES SHREDDED MOZZARELLA CHEESE

CHOPPED FRESH BASIL, FOR GARNISH

1. Preheat the oven to 400°F.

2. Spread half of the marinara sauce in the bottom of a 13 x 9-inch casserole dish or any deep oven-safe dish.

3. With the spiralizer on setting 2, spiralize the onion into thin strips and lay the slices evenly over the marinara sauce.

4. Trim the ends off the yellow squash and zucchini. With the spiralizer on setting 1, spiralize them into ribbons. Spread the ribbons evenly across the entire dish.

5. Slice the tomatoes and eggplant into 1-inch cubes and fit them in within the ribbons.

6. Season the dish with the red wine vinegar, dried basil, oregano and salt and pepper to taste. Add the remaining half of the marinara sauce on top of the vegetables.

7. Cover the dish with foil and bake the casserole for 30 minutes.

8. Remove the foil after 30 minutes and sprinkle the shredded mozzarella on top. Return the casserole to the oven and bake for another 10 to 15 minutes, or until the cheese is lightly browned.

9. Allow the casserole to rest for 5 minutes after removing it from the oven. Garnish with the chopped fresh basil and serve.

**EAT WELL** *with Ming*

USING A VARIETY OF VEGETABLES IN THIS CASSEROLE BOOSTS NUTRIENT INTAKE AND KEEPS THE FLAVOR INTERESTING. EGGPLANT NOT ONLY INTRODUCES A NEW PURPLE COLOR INTO THE MIX, BUT DID YOU KNOW THAT ONE MEDIUM EGGPLANT HAS MORE THAN 50% OF YOUR DAILY FIBER NEEDS?

# Butternut Squash NOODLE QUICHE WITH SAUSAGE

A QUICHE IS AN EASY WAY to feed a crowd with one dish at any meal. In this version, a sweet butternut squash crust cradles creamy eggs paired with sausage, onions and mushrooms and accented with garlic, basil and oregano.

CRUST

1 LARGE BUTTERNUT SQUASH

4 TABLESPOONS UNSALTED BUTTER, AT ROOM TEMPERATURE

1 LARGE EGG

FILLING

12 OUNCES SWEET ITALIAN SAUSAGES

1 TABLESPOON OLIVE OIL

1/2 MEDIUM YELLOW ONION, CHOPPED2 CLOVES GARLIC, MINCED

1/2 TEASPOON DRIED BASIL

1/2 TEASPOON DRIED OREGANO

8 OUNCES WHITE MUSHROOMS, SLICED

10 LARGE EGGS

SALT AND PEPPER

FRESH BASIL, FOR GARNISH

1. Preheat the oven to 375°F.

2. To make the crust, cut off the bulbous half of the butternut squash. Cut the end of the straighter half off and peel its hard skin multiple times until you reach the bright orange inside. With the spiralizer on setting 4, spiralize the squash into thin noodles.

3. In a large mixing bowl, combine the softened butter, egg and butternut squash noodles.

4. Press the squash noodles into a 9-inch pie dish until you have an even thickness on both the bottom and the sides. Transfer the pie dish to the oven and bake the crust for 20 minutes.

5. In the meantime, to make the filling, remove the sausages from their casings.

6. Heat the olive oil in a skillet over medium heat and cook the sausages for about 4 minutes, breaking up the sausage meat with a wooden spoon into small chunks.

7. Remove the sausage from the pan and place in a bowl, and then add the chopped onion, garlic, dried basil and oregano to the pan. Cook them for about 5 minutes, or until the onion is softened.

8. Add the mushrooms and cook for another 3 minutes. Remove the pan from the heat.

9. Once the crust is ready, add the sautéed vegetables and sausage on top. Spread everything out evenly so the surface of the crust is fully covered.

10. Whisk the eggs and salt and pepper to taste in a bowl and pour the mixture over the sausage and vegetables.

11. Return the quiche to the oven and bake for 25 minutes, or until the eggs are set. Place on a wire rack to cool for 5 minutes.

12. Garnish the quiche with the chopped fresh basil, cut into slices and serve.

## EAT WELL *with Ming*

MAKING A QUICHE IS A PERFECT WAY TO USE UP LEFTOVER VEGETABLES AND CREATE A MEAL THAT'S SURE TO KEEP YOU FULL FOR HOURS! USE THE VEGETABLES WE LIST OR SUB IN OTHERS THAT ARE MORE TAILORED TO YOUR FAMILY'S TASTES.

# SPIRALIZED
# SIDES

# BUTTERNUT SQUASH FRITTERS *with Herb Butter*

THESE FRITTERS PACK BOTH SWEET AND SAVORY into one bite! To speed prep time as a dinner side, prepare the herb butter the day before making the fritters.

---

**HERB BUTTER**

5 OR 6 FRESH BASIL LEAVES

2 FRESH MINT LEAVES

1 BUNCH FRESH TARRAGON

1 BUNCH FRESH PARSLEY

8 TABLESPOONS (1/2 CUP OR 1 STICK) UNSALTED BUTTER, AT ROOM TEMPERATURE

1/2 TEASPOON SEA SALT

**FRITTERS**

2 TO 3 CUPS AVOCADO OIL

2 BUTTERNUT SQUASH

2 CLOVES GARLIC

1 LARGE EGG

2 TABLESPOONS COCONUT FLOUR

SALT AND PEPPER

1. To make the herb butter, mince the herbs finely and add them to a small bowl. Add the softened butter and salt, and stir to thoroughly combine the ingredients.

2. Add the butter mixture to a sheet of plastic wrap and roll it tightly into a log shape. Refrigerate it overnight so it will be ready for the fritters the next day.

3. To make the fritters, heat the avocado oil (or any mild-tasting oil with a high smoke point, like coconut oil) in a small pot over high heat while you prepare the batter.

4. Cut off the bulbous half of the butternut squash. Cut the end of the straighter half off and peel its hard skin multiple times until you reach the bright orange inside. With the spiralizer on setting 4, spiralize the butternut squash into thin noodles and place them in a deep mixing bowl.

5. Run some kitchen shears through the noodles a few times to cut them into shorter strands. This will help the patties stay a uniform size.

6. Use a garlic press to squeeze the garlic cloves into the butternut squash noodles.

7. Add the egg and coconut flour. If you don't have coconut flour, use your favorite gluten-free flour, though you may need to use a bit more of it.

8. Season with salt and pepper and use your hands to coat the noodles and mix everything together until all the noodles are covered in a batterlike coating.

9. Take a handful of noodles and squeeze them into flat patties 4 to 5 inches in diameter. You should get 8 patties.

10. Test the oil by dipping a strand of noodle into it. If it sizzles after more than 1 to 2 seconds, the oil is not hot enough. Or use a thermometer to test the heat; it should be 375°F.

11. Lower in 1 butternut squash fritter at a time and let it fry for about 6 minutes. Toward the end, flip it over a few times to prevent one side from frying and browning too much.

12. Transfer the fritter to a paper towel–lined plate to drain and repeat the process with the rest of the fritters.

13. Add 1 tablespoon of the herb butter to each fritter and serve.

## EAT WELL *with Ming*

AVOCADO OIL CONTAINS MONOUNSATURATED FAT, THE KIND CONSIDERED TO BE HEART-HEALTHY. IT'S USEFUL IN COOKING AND DELICIOUS WHEN ADDED TO SALAD DRESSINGS.

# *Jicama* HASH BROWNS

JICAMA IS A ROOT VEGETABLE that works well as a substitute for potatoes in recipes. Enjoy these Jicama Hash Browns as a dinner side with a traditional entrée or (even better!) breakfast for dinner.

---

1 LARGE JICAMA

1 LARGE EGG, BEATEN

2 TABLESPOONS
COCONUT FLOUR

1 TEASPOON PAPRIKA

PINCH OF CAYENNE
(OPTIONAL)

SALT AND PEPPER

2 TABLESPOONS
UNSALTED BUTTER,
PLUS MORE
FOR SERVING

1. Slice the ends off the jicama and carefully cut the waxy skin off with a paring knife. With the spiralizer on setting 4, spiralize the jicama into thin noodles.

2. In a medium bowl, combine the noodles with the egg and coconut flour and use your hands to mix and coat everything evenly.

3. Season the mixture with the paprika, cayenne (if using) and salt and pepper to taste.

4. Mix everything once again and, using your hands, start forming flat, round patties about 2 inches in diameter.

5. Heat the butter in a frying pan over medium heat until slightly browned, then fry each hash brown for about 5 minutes on each side. The outsides of the hash browns should be browned and crispy, while the insides should remain soft.

6. Serve the Jicama Hash Browns hot with an extra smear of butter.

## EAT WELL *with Ming*

JICAMA IS PACKED WITH VITAMIN C AND $B_6$ AND OFFERS A HEALTHY DOSE OF IRON AS WELL.

# Mexican Jicama
# NOODLE SALAD

JICAMA WORKS GREAT IN SALADS AND SALSAS, lending a slightly sweet crunch that doesn't lose crispness over time. Though it isn't much to look at, it tastes like a delicious cross between an apple and an Asian pear.

1 LARGE JICAMA

½ RED ONION, DICED

4 CAMPARI TOMATOES, DICED

2 AVOCADOS, PITTED, PEELED AND DICED

1 JALAPEÑO (OPTIONAL)

JUICE OF 1 LIME

2 TABLESPOONS OLIVE OIL

SALT AND PEPPER

CHOPPED FRESH CILANTRO, FOR GARNISH

1. Slice the ends off the jicama and carefully cut off the waxy skin with a paring knife. With the spiralizer on setting 3, spiralize the jicama into thick noodles.

2. Combine the red onion, tomatoes and avocados with the jicama noodles in a large bowl.

3. If using the jalapeño, dice it and add it to the bowl. Remove the seeds and white membranes for less heat.

4. Add the lime juice, olive oil and salt and pepper to taste and toss the salad to combine.

5. Garnish with the cilantro and serve.

## EAT WELL with Ming

JICAMA IS A VERSATILE VEGETABLE THAT IS INCREDIBLY CRUNCHY AND DELICIOUS. DID YOU KNOW IT'S A GOOD SOURCE OF FIBER?

# *Golden* BEET SALAD

JUST SEVEN SIMPLE INGREDIENTS create a complement of earthy, sweet and tart flavors in this Golden Beet Salad. Sunflower seeds add delicious and nutritious crunch.

**SALAD**

2 GOLDEN BEETS (OR REGULAR BEETS)

4 CUPS FRESH ARUGULA

1/2 RED ONION, SLICED

1/4 CUP SUNFLOWER SEEDS

**DRESSING**

1/2 CUP FULL-FAT GREEK YOGURT

2 TABLESPOONS HONEY

SALT

1. To make the salad, trim any leaves and stems off the golden beets and peel them. Use gloves to prevent your fingers from staining. With the spiralizer on setting 2, 3 or 4, spiralize the beets into thin or thick noodles according to your preference.

2. Add the beet noodles to a mixing bowl along with the arugula.

3. Add the sliced red onion and sunflower seeds.

4. To make the dressing, whisk together the Greek yogurt, honey and salt in a small bowl.

5. Drizzle the dressing over the salad, divide it among 4 plates and serve.

**EAT WELL** *with Ming*

USING FULL-FAT GREEK YOGURT HELPS KEEP YOU FULL LONGER. THE INGREDIENT IS ALSO LOADED WITH MINERALS SUCH AS PHOSPHORUS, WHICH IS IMPORTANT FOR BONE HEALTH.

# Rainbow RIBBONS SALAD

SO MANY COLORFUL VEGETABLES, so much fresh flavor and texture! Make your taste buds and nutritionists everywhere happy.

2 MEDIUM ZUCCHINI

2 YELLOW SQUASH

2 MEDIUM CARROTS

1 HEAD OF RED CABBAGE

4 CAMPARI TOMATOES, DICED

TAHINI DRESSING
¼ CUP TAHINI

2 TEASPOONS HONEY

JUICE OF ½ LIME

2 CLOVES GARLIC

1 TEASPOON GRATED GINGER

2 TABLESPOONS OLIVE OIL

2 TABLESPOONS WATER

SALT AND PEPPER

SESAME SEEDS, FOR GARNISH

1. Trim the ends off the zucchini, yellow squash and carrots and peel the carrots. With the spiralizer on setting 4, spiralize all three vegetables into thin noodles. Add the noodles to a large bowl.

2. With the spiralizer on setting 1, shred the red cabbage and add it to the bowl along with the diced tomatoes.

3. To make the tahini dressing, add the tahini, honey, lime juice, garlic, ginger, oil, water and salt and pepper to taste to a food processor and blend the ingredients until you get a smooth consistency.

4. Dress the salad with the tahini dressing and toss to combine everything well.

5. Garnish with the sesame seeds and serve.

## EAT WELL with Ming

ZUCCHINI ARE A GREAT SOURCE OF COPPER, A TRACE MINERAL NEEDED TO HELP IRON FORM RED BLOOD CELLS.

# *Minted* CUCUMBER SALAD

MINTED CUCUMBER SALAD is a perfect light accompaniment to any dinner recipe. Cucumber and mint add refreshing flavor mixed with a touch of tang from yogurt.

---

2 LARGE CUCUMBERS

1/4 CUP CHOPPED
RED ONION

1/2 CUP FULL-FAT
GREEK YOGURT

5 OR 6 LARGE FRESH
MINT LEAVES, PLUS
1 FOR GARNISH

1/2 TEASPOON SEA SALT

1/2 TEASPOON DRIED DILL

2 TABLESPOONS
OLIVE OIL

1/2 TABLESPOON
WHITE VINEGAR

1. With the spiralizer on setting 1, spiralize the cucumbers into ribbons and add them to a mixing bowl.

2. Add the chopped red onion and yogurt and toss to combine.

3. Roughly chop the mint leaves and add them to the mixing bowl along with the salt, dill, olive oil and vinegar. Toss well to combine and garnish with a fresh mint leaf.

## EAT WELL *with Ming*

USING FULL-FAT GREEK YOGURT PACKS IN PROTEIN AND HELPS KEEP YOU FULL LONGER!

# DELICIOUS DESSERTS

# *Apple* CRISP

DON'T SPEND ALL YOUR TIME CHOPPING! You can make homemade Apple Crisp with less effort when you put your spiralizer to work for you.

CRUMB TOPPING
1/2 CUP ALL-PURPOSE FLOUR

1/2 CUP OLD-FASHIONED OATS

1/2 CUP BROWN SUGAR

1/4 TEASPOONS GROUND CINNAMON

DASH OF SALT

1/3 CUP UNSALTED BUTTER, DICED INTO SMALL CHUNKS

APPLE FILLING
3 OR 4 LARGE GRANNY SMITH APPLES, CORED AND PEELED

3 TABLESPOONS UNSALTED BUTTER, MELTED

2 TABLESPOONS ALL-PURPOSE FLOUR

1 TABLESPOON LEMON JUICE

1/2 TEASPOON VANILLA EXTRACT

1/4 CUP BROWN SUGAR

1/2 TEASPOON GROUND CINNAMON

DASH OF SALT

VANILLA ICE CREAM, FOR SERVING (OPTIONAL)

1. Preheat the oven to 375°F.

2. To make the topping, in a medium bowl, combine with a fork or pastry blender the flour, oats, brown sugar, cinnamon, salt and butter until the mixture resembles small crumbs. Refrigerate while you prepare the apple filling.

3. To make the apple filling, with the spiralizer on setting 3, spiralize the apples into thick noodles.

4. In a small bowl, combine the melted butter and flour until well blended. Add the lemon juice and vanilla extract, and stir well. Stir in the brown sugar, cinnamon and salt.

5. Pour the butter mixture over the apples and toss to coat.

6. Pour the apple mixture into an 8 x 8-inch baking dish and spread into an even layer. Sprinkle the crumb topping evenly over the apples. Bake for 30 to 35 minutes, or until golden brown and the top is set.

7. Remove from the oven and allow to cool for at least 10 minutes before serving with vanilla ice cream, if desired.

**EAT WELL** *with Ming*

GRANNY SMITH APPLES ARE PACKED WITH FIBER, WHICH CAN HELP YOU FEEL FULL LONGER. THEY'RE A DELICIOUS SNACK ALONE OR A FLAVORFUL ADDITION TO RECIPES.

# APPLE *Turnovers*

NO ROLLING PIN REQUIRED! Puff pastry helps you envelope your spiralized apples in light, flaky goodness.

1/3 CUP GRANULATED SUGAR

1 TABLESPOON ALL-PURPOSE FLOUR

1/2 TEASPOON GROUND CINNAMON

3 MEDIUM APPLES, PEELED AND CORED

1 TEASPOON LEMON JUICE

1 (17.3-OUNCE) PACKAGE PUFF PASTRY SHEETS, THAWED

1 TABLESPOON UNSALTED BUTTER, MELTED

GLAZE

1 CUP CONFECTIONER'S SUGAR

1 TABLESPOON WATER OR MILK

1. Preheat the oven to 400°F. Line a baking sheet with parchment paper.

2. In a large bowl, whisk together the granulated sugar, flour and cinnamon.

3. With the spiralizer on setting 3, spiralize the apples into thick noodles.

4. Add the apples and lemon juice to the sugar mixture, and toss to coat evenly. Set aside.

5. On a lightly floured surface, roll out the pastry sheets. Cut each into 4 squares. Place the squares on the baking sheet.

6. Spoon about ¼ cup of the apple mixture into the corner half of each square and fold to make a triangle. Press the edges together, then crimp with a fork. Brush the tops of each turnover with the melted butter.

7. Bake for 16 to 20 minutes, or until golden brown.

8. Meanwhile, to make the glaze, stir together the confectioner's sugar and water until smooth.

9. Drizzle the glaze over the turnovers before serving.

## EAT WELL *with Ming*

CHOOSE TREATS THAT COME IN INDIVIDUAL SERVINGS FOR BETTER PORTION CONTROL.

# *Spiralized*
# STRAWBERRY SORBET

MOST SORBETS NEED LOTS OF CARE and attention as they freeze—often scraping with a fork every so often. But you can get the same flavor and texture by putting your spiralizer to work.

---

**3 CUPS WATER**

**1 CUP SUGAR**

**3 CUPS FROZEN STRAWBERRIES**

**2 TEASPOONS GRATED LEMON ZEST**

1. In a medium saucepan over high heat, bring the water and sugar just to a boil, stirring until the sugar dissolves. Remove from the heat; cool.

2. Process the sugar syrup, strawberries and zest, in batches, in a blender or food processor until smooth.

3. Place the mixture in paper cups and freeze until solid.

4. Remove the sorbet by simply peeling away the cups. Before serving, spiralize the sorbet on setting 1.

**EAT WELL** *with Ming*

FROZEN FRUIT IS A SMART OPTION WHEN GOOD, RIPE PRODUCE ISN'T AVAILABLE. FRUITS THAT WILL BE FROZEN ARE GENERALLY PICKED AT PEAK RIPENESS, WHEN THEY'RE THE MOST NUTRITIOUS.

# SPIRALIZED
# CANTALOUPE *Sorbet*

NOTHING IS MORE REFRESHING than summer fruit sorbet! Here's a new twist on a classic recipe.

---

**3 CUPS WATER**  **1 CUP SUGAR**  **4 CUPS CHOPPED CANTALOUPE**

1. In a medium saucepan over high heat, bring the water and sugar just to a boil, stirring until the sugar dissolves. Remove from the heat; cool.

2. Process the sugar syrup and cantaloupe, in batches, in a blender or food processor until smooth.

3. Place the mixture in paper cups and freeze until solid.

4. Remove the sorbet by simply peeling away the cups. Before serving, spiralize the sorbet on setting 1.

**EAT WELL** *with Ming*

CANTALOUPE IS AN EXCELLENT SOURCE OF VITAMIN A, A POWERFUL ANTIOXIDANT THAT'S IMPORTANT FOR VISION AND SKIN HEALTH.

# *Pear* BREAD PUDDING

PEARS MAKE THE PERFECT, festive fall dessert with fewer than ten ingredients. A little time to chill and set helps the bread really soak up the flavors.

1 (16- TO 20-OUNCE) LOAF BREAD OR BRIOCHE (10 TO 12 CUPS BREAD CUBES)

1 TABLESPOON UNSALTED BUTTER, SOFTENED

5 CUPS WHOLE MILK

6 LARGE EGGS

1 CUP SUGAR

2 TEASPOONS VANILLA EXTRACT

1 TEASPOON GROUND CINNAMON

1/8 TEASPOON SALT

2 BOSC PEARS, PEELED AND CORED

1. Preheat the oven to 350°F. Butter a 9 x 13-inch baking dish.

2. Slice the bread into bite-size cubes, or tear it into pieces with your hands. Remove the crust from the bread, if desired; leave it on for a more rustic dessert.

3. Spread the bread cubes in a single layer on a baking sheet. Toast for 20 to 25 minutes, stirring once halfway through cooking, until the cubes feel dry and hard but are still very pale. Remove from the oven and cool slightly.

4. Transfer the cubes evenly to the prepared baking dish.

5. Whisk together the milk, eggs, sugar, vanilla, cinnamon and salt in a mixing bowl.

6. With the spiralizer on setting 4, spiralize the pear into thin noodles. Add the pear to the egg mixture.

7. Gently fold the egg mixture into the bread. Refrigerate for 1 hour.

8. Preheat the oven to 350°F.

9. Bake the bread pudding for 45 minutes, or until golden brown.

EAT WELL *with Ming* ———————

DID YOU KNOW PEARS ARE ONE OF THE MOST POPULAR FRUITS IN THE WORLD? IT'S NO WONDER—THEY'RE PACKED WITH SWEET, JUICY FLAVOR AND VITAMIN C.

# ALPHABETICAL LIST OF RECIPES

# METRIC CONVERSIONS

## VOLUME

| US | METRIC |
|---|---|
| 1/8 TEASPOON | 0.5 MILLILITERS |
| 1/4 TEASPOON | 1 MILLILITERS |
| 1/2 TEASPOON | 2 MILLILITERS |
| 3/4 TEASPOON | 4 MILLILITERS |
| 1 TEASPOON | 5 MILLILITERS |
| 1 TABLESPOON | 15 MILLILITERS |
| 1/4 CUP | 60 MILLILITERS |
| 1/3 CUP | 80 MILLILITERS |
| 1/2 CUP | 120 MILLILITERS |
| 2/3 CUP | 160 MILLILITERS |
| 3/4 CUP | 180 MILLILITERS |
| 1 CUP | 225 MILLILITERS (DRY), 250 MILLILITERS (LIQUID) |
| 2 CUPS (1 PINT) | 450 MILLILITERS, 500 MILLILITERS (LIQUID) |
| 4 CUPS (1 QUART) | 1 LITER |
| 1/2 GALLON | 2 LITERS |
| 1 GALLON | 4 LITERS |

## WEIGHT

| US | METRIC |
|---|---|
| 1 OUNCE | 28 GRAMS |
| 4 OUNCES (1/4 POUND) | 113 GRAMS |
| 8 OUNCES (1/2 POUND) | 230 GRAMS |
| 12 OUNCES (3/4 POUND) | 340 GRAMS |
| 16 OUNCES (1 POUND) | 450 GRAMS |
| 23 OUNCES (2 POUNDS) | 900 GRAMS |

## LENGTH

| US | METRIC |
|---|---|
| 1/4 INCH | 6 MILLIMETERS |
| 1/2 INCH | 13 MILLIMETERS |
| 3/4 INCH | 19 MILLIMETERS |
| 1 INCH | 2 1/2 CENTIMETERS |
| 1 1/2 INCHES | 3 3/4 CENTIMETERS |
| 2 INCHES | 5 CENTIMETERS |
| 2 1/2 INCHES | 6 1/2 CENTIMETERS |

## TEMPERATURES

| FAHRENHEIT | CELSIUS |
|---|---|
| 250°F | 120°C |
| 275°F | 140°C |
| 300°F | 150°C |
| 325°F | 170°C |
| 350°F | 180°C |
| 375°F | 190°C |
| 400°F | 200°C |
| 425°F | 220°C |
| 450°F | 230°C |
| 475°F | 240°C |
| 500°F | 260°C |